the Art of
BELIEVING
on
PURPOSE

Life Changing Reflections

from

The Deep Dive Coach

Bev Aron

For the two women who are always present as
I live my bold and beautiful life -

In memory of my mother,
Renée Aron ʓ,
for showing me the power of healing conversations

Brooke Castillo,
for teaching me how to offer them

To stay informed about upcoming
Bev Aron publications contact:
www.bevaron.com

Publication Design and Illustrations
David Brady
Brady Book Design
www.bradybookdesign.com

Photos
Danielle Cohen
www.danielle-cohen.com

Printed in the United States.

Introduction

I asked my son, who was one of my editors, what he thought about The Art of Believing on Purpose, and he told me that he'd read most of the ideas before. He's right. I'm not an originator of ideas, and I don't need to be. All the knowledge we need to live fulfilling lives is available to us and has been described eloquently in numerous books. Yet, the ability to live and benefit from the belief that we are in control of our life continues to elude most people, despite many instructional guidebooks on the topic. This book is different.

The most common question my life coach students and clients ask me is "How?" How do I believe on purpose to create the results I want? How do you do it? How do I start? This book is my answer to those questions. I describe small, everyday moments and share how my clients, students and I use the power of our minds to change our experience of these moments. My hope is that you feel equipped to experiment and discover ways to create magic in your life. There's no right or wrong way to do this, and it's rarely neat. It's a conscious decision, moment by moment, to believe that you have everything you need now to live the life you want to live, no matter what is happening around you. It's not dramatic. It's usually quiet and subtle. Often you're the only one who notices. And that's all you need. Creating a life that you dream of is the sum of deliberately practicing beliefs during your everyday moments – the ones that challenge you and that you would prefer weren't happening.

You will notice recurring themes woven throughout the chapters. These are my challenging moments – yoga, running, and keeping my commitments. They will differ from your themes, and that is as it should be. Believing on purpose is an art, and your art will be uniquely yours based on what you want to believe on purpose to create the life you yearn to live.

The Art of Believing on Purpose is less about figuring out how to be the version of yourself that will satisfy the rest of the world (hint: there's no version of you—or anyone else—that will satisfy the rest of the world) and more about figuring out how to accept who you are in spite of, or dare I suggest, because of the parts that make you the beautiful human you are.

DEEPER WISDOM WITH YOU

This book is an invitation for you to explore the deeper wisdom that resides within you. I've compiled my thoughts and reflections about how I've pushed through my own challenges and learned to accept my own version of full-frontal chaotic living. But I don't have all the answers. At no point did I wake up and think, "I've got everything figured out." Nor am I suggesting everything that has worked for my clients or me will work for you. Anyone who has worked hard to learn how to believe in herself understands that we aren't looking for a cure or a quick fix. Discovering how to tap into this inner wisdom is an ongoing process, an unfolding of the self over time. And I hope that these reflections will serve as inspiration for all those looking to do their own work.

In front of you is a collection of brief reflections written over many years. I invite you to make this book your own and use it to enhance your mindfulness and self-reflection practices.

There are several ways you could use this book:

Read it through cover-to-cover by yourself or with others.

Read an individual section as it applies to your present moment to find comfort or inspiration.

Read a single reflection to set the tone for meditation or a few moments of stillness.

Use a single reflection as a journaling prompt.

Simply let your intuition guide you to the message you need to read today.

However you use this book, I hope it serves as a reminder of the love and compassion that exists all around you. When you choose to believe on purpose, you will be amazed at how ordinary moments naturally become magical, enchanting occasions.

You do have full over your life.

Do you know how much your unconscious choices are affecting your life?

Choosing your choices sounds obvious, but I want to invite you to question and observe yourself making decisions. I'm guessing, based on my work with hundreds of independent and intelligent adults, that you attribute the majority of your choices to other people and events. I hope that as you read the reflections in this chapter, you will start to see how much power you hold in how you live your life, no matter what happens around you.

It's curious how we absolve ourselves of responsibility for all the choices we make in our lives, while at the same time we yearn to feel in control and empowered and strong. What we don't realize is that we already are. Living in a free world, as adults, we are always choosing, and the most powerful decision you can make in your quest to live from strength and wisdom is to dive deeply into the source of your choices, one by one, and realize that all of your decisions are caused by your own thoughts.

Let's imagine that we're hovering above your body together, you and I, as you go about your day, winking at each other every time we notice you pretending you didn't choose your response to a given moment, when of course you did. Start with the small moments – the ones I describe in this chapter: a substitute fitness instructor, lost luggage, or heavy traffic.

control As you read the following reflections, consider where in your life you want to make conscious choices. Choosing your choices means that you use the power of your mind to create your life intentionally. Do this often enough, and you will develop the habit of choosing your choices, instead of reacting and then blaming your choices on the people and events in your life.

THINK DIFFERENTLY ——————

How long until you choose to feel better?

In my experience, if we choose what we really want, it doesn't take long to change our thinking and the type of resistance our brains create. Sometimes, just knowing that one person is doing it is all it takes for another person to decide to do it too. Consider the following examples:

One morning I was out running, and as I turned the corner, an acquaintance opened her window to say, "I love you."
Life just keeps getting better, I thought.

She went on to tell me that she had hurt her leg during power yoga and instead of quitting, she remembered what I'd said about falling and continuing to run instead of using it as a valid excuse to quit.
(read more on page 85).

My story inspired her to continue the class, and although she found it painful initially, by the end of the class, she felt energized, powerful, and strong.

A few weeks earlier, a former student thanked me. Her father had died right before Father's Day, and as she thought about what to do that Sunday, she told herself that she had a choice—she could be sad or she could celebrate his life.

She asked herself, "What would Bev do?", which led her to have a big BBQ and celebrate an amazing Father's Day with her husband, children, and extended family.

What do you need to do to give yourself permission to choose to feel better? Try these:

Think differently.

Look at whatever happens positively.

Choose to celebrate, even when sad things happen.

Test your strength and see how far you can go even when conventional wisdom says you've done enough.

Love your body no matter what.

Don't care if other people think you're too much, or too little, or too braggy.

Decide you are lovable, even if no one else tells you so.

Decide how you will perceive an event, regardless of how everyone else is perceiving it.

Choose peace, even if everyone else is fighting.

How can you be so happy all the time?

Twelve hours into a road trip, my seven-year-old asked me, "Mommy, how can you be so happy all the time?"

Her question surprised me.
I hadn't even thought about it – I was really happy.

I was having the best day with my whole family in one place, playing games, listening to music, laughing, and having long meandering conversations. No one was distracted by the TV, computer, phone, plans, or work. It was a bubble of warmth. Pure happiness. In a car.

I told her that I chose to be happy by the way I think. I'd been thinking about how much I love my family and how grateful I was that we were having an amazing holiday.

Her question reminded me of how I used to be on long road trips. I hated them. I complained the entire time. I would have tantrums in anticipation of the kids having tantrums, being bored, or getting hungry. In fact, for years my husband would drive with two kids, and I would fly with two kids. He loves long drives because he thinks they're relaxing and enjoyable.

I used to believe I got the better deal. I had many thoughts about how it was too long to drive, too boring to sit for so long, too hard to keep the kids entertained. I hated passing them food all the time. I didn't want to listen to their complaints and fighting. Disney World (one of their stops) was too loud, too busy, too fake. I thought driving to Florida was too "middle America" for unique me!

But I noticed that when they picked us up at the airport, they were already relaxed and tanned. We, the fliers, were still stressed, achy, and pasty. Plus, they always had all their luggage with them!

Following a discussion with my coach I decided that driving should be a family event. I worked hard to convince my husband. The deal was that I would be a passive passenger—no decision-making powers and no opinions—which is different from my usual role in our family.

I packed fresh fruit and veggies, knitting, needlepoint, and a laptop. I felt lucky to have been let into this exclusive little club. I was excited to discover what there was to see and to explore new territory. And guess what? l loved it. We were creating family memories, and I was well behaved (and by the way, so were the kids) because I was happy.

What changed?
The circumstance stayed exactly the same: 24-hour drive to Florida over two days. Results: totally different.

How?
Because my thinking about the drive changed, my feelings changed, so my actions changed, which resulted in our entire family experience being rewritten.

It's a wonderful thing that I decided to invest in coaching before my kids were old enough to remember their tantrummy Mama—maybe with time, my hubby will also forget that I wasn't always "happy all the time."

There's nowhere else I'd rather be

You may think it's easy for me to tell you that there's nowhere else on earth I'd rather be, as I write this from my beachfront vacation with my husband.

But I choose this thought ALWAYS. No matter what is happening, I can always find it.

Initially, it was a conscious decision to think this, and then find how it is true for me, but now it just burbles up in me, and I am always EXACTLY where I want to be.

I'm not saying I always find myself where I planned to be. Like the time my Lululemon returns took longer than I anticipated because the cashier was new. I'm not proud that I didn't choose to be gracious to her. But still, I knew that there was nowhere else on earth I'd rather be because it showed me that I still have inner work to do on my responses to events I would prefer were different.

Would I rather have been on the bike trail that morning? No.

If I had wanted to be biking already, I would have been.

Don't say, "I don't want to make my kids lunch every day."

Of course you do. Otherwise, you wouldn't do it.

"But then, they'd be hungry at school, the school would call me, and they'd be miserable when they got home."

Ah. You do want to make their lunches because you like collecting happy kids and you prefer days when the school doesn't call. Good to know— making lunch is EXACTLY where you want to be every morning.

I know that you can give me many reasons you don't want to be where you are—

"Work's a drag"

"Sitting in a car that isn't moving on a busy road sucks"
"My husband is yelling at me, and it's hurting my head"

I've heard all of these, and I've thought a few of them, too.
(Thankfully, my husband doesn't yell).
I hear you.

And I know it's easy to find these reasons and you'd love to convince me about all of it.

But thinking this way doesn't feel good, does it?
I just want to tell you that it's a choice.

I'm not suggesting that you paper over your complaints with pretty "life-is-wonderful-and-perfect" thoughts. Those never work, unless we believe them.

I am recommending that you wholeheartedly commit to truly FINDING how you are always exactly where you want to be in every moment—

"I want to be at work because I love earning my own money."

"I want to be in this car on the way to dinner with my friends."

"I want to be in my home with my husband who I love and who loves me when things are hard and good and all of it in between— if I didn't want to be here, I wouldn't be here."

Sometimes it's hard to look because we discover that we want to be here only because we are afraid of leaving. That's challenging, but important, because now you know where your work is.

Can you change your feelings without changing your situation?

Recently, a family in my community was suffering, and I had volunteered to prepare dinner for them. I hardly knew this family and didn't feel any connection to them.

I started my cooking session ambitiously – chopping, peeling, dicing, mincing, sautéing, and slicing. But once I became aware of the scope of the project and the mounds of unfinished tasks in my home, I became resentful.

I consider even one minute lived in 'resentfulness' to be a wasted minute of my life. And I consider my life way too precious and exciting to waste. So I decided to coach myself.

I traced the feeling of resentfulness to the thoughts that were causing it, and they weren't admirable:

"I don't even know these people."

"She won't even thank me."

"She probably won't even know who it's from."

"Why didn't I just order in for them?"

"I have so much to do."

YUCK? I agree.

My next step was to change my thinking in order to feel better. I found a new thought: "This family is providing me with an opportunity to practice pure giving."

How did this thought make me feel?

Grateful.
Instant gratitude.
I have to admit, I was dazzled by this thought!

How did changing my thoughts and feelings change my afternoon?

I proceeded calmly in gratitude:

For the fresh, life-giving food I was working with.

For this free afternoon.

For the cherry blossoms outside my kitchen window.

For the birds chirping outside.

For the chance to send this family a delicious, nutritious meal.

TRACE THE FEELING

I doubled the recipe, turned up the volume, danced, and sang as I sliced, chopped, diced, sautéed, peeled, minced, and mixed.

I arrived just in time to deliver the meal and returned home grateful for the delicious, nutritious meal waiting for my family.
And that's the power of thinking on purpose.

It didn't change a thing about my afternoon and yet it changed everything.

What thought barriers can you break today?

I love the story of the four-minute mile. Do you know it?
Until 1954, no one had been known to run a mile in under four minutes. All the fastest runners tried and tried and couldn't do it. Until Roger Bannister did. Suddenly, all those elite runners who had failed were running a mile in four minutes or less.
So what changed?

Not their physical ability.
Their thinking changed.

Before, they thought it was physically impossible, so it was - for them.
Now, they knew it was possible, so it was – for them.

Peace was always available to us.

The women in my goal-oriented coaching groups do it daily.
Every time they tell me they can't give something up, or start something new, I invite them to question this thinking.

I show them that it's true they can't, but only because they think they can't.

Sometimes they decide to believe may be able to do it and immediately feel more open. Because we're in a group, some who have done it share their experience and how wonderful they feel. Suddenly it becomes a possibility for the others.

We give up caffeine, diet soda, Netflix, alcohol, conflict with in-laws.
We say no to Facebook, dessert, chocolate, and the belief that we must do it perfectly. What we gain is lightness, energy, vitality, ease, peace.

This peace, of course, was always available to us.
But because we believed that it wasn't, it wasn't.

Now that we're practicing believing it is possible no matter what's happening around us, we're discovering that it is.
Have fun with this. I invite you to:

*Notice one belief that is only true for you because you believe that it is.

*And invite yourself to blast through that thought barrier and see what you find on the other side.

What are you missing out on because you think you can't do it?

We create our own reality by always taking actions that provide evidence for our thoughts. The impact of this is that when we convince ourselves that we won't succeed, we miss out on many opportunities.

I have always thought that I am the worst athlete alive. The proof I carried with me was my experience in high school Phys. Ed. class. The basketball team captains were my two best friends, and yet I was picked last. Every week. Of every year.
I haven't touched a ball since.

So you will understand my dilemma when my husband invited me to join him and some friends for a casual game of beach volleyball.
I said, "No."
He was disappointed.
I explained why.
He was understanding.
And disappointed.

And then, LIGHTBULB! I remembered that I'm a coach and I know how to manage my thoughts!

I chose to think, "Maybe I CAN do this."

I also tried, "I'm willing to suck at beach volleyball because I want to connect with my husband and his friends."

Lastly, I offered myself, "Maybe it will be fun."

These thoughts took me from tight, resistant and guilty to loose, light and open.

And guess what?
All my thoughts came true, as they usually do.
That night I proved:

Maybe I could do this one day (but that wasn't the day,
although my sweet husband assures me I made two
saves and my last serve nearly went over the net).

I was willing to suck (and I did).

I wanted to connect with my husband and his friends
and I definitely did.

IT WAS DEFINITELY FUN!

We all have the tools to turn a situation where we are missing out
because of our limiting thoughts into an opportunity to use the power
of our conscious thinking to open ourselves to a new experience.

Imagine if I'd known this skill when I was in high school. Maybe one
of my best friends would have picked me, if I hadn't been hiding in the
shadows thinking (and proving), "No one ever picks me."

MAYBE I CAN DO THIS

What are you thinking? And how's it making you feel?

My regular Group Power fitness instructor was unexpectedly replaced
by a woman who ran the class in slow motion. I was still able to have a
good workout—of my mind. My muscles, not much, unfortunately.

I spent the first ten minutes scowling at her while she ambled in three
minutes late, slowly set up the music, blew her nose, introduced
herself, and prepared her equipment.

After each set of ten reps, we stretched the muscle we were (supposed
to be) working. Mostly, I worked my frown muscles big time.

Eventually, I noticed that my body was tight. I was feeling irritated.

Cheated.
Which led to me to glare at the teacher, mutter to my classmate,
interrupt the teacher to ask her to up the intensity of the class, and
generally spoil my own experience.

My mind wandered, and I thought:

"She's wasting my precious time."

"I don't have another hour to get a proper workout in."

"This is not a seniors' class."

"They should've warned me that Tonya wouldn't be teaching today."

"They shouldn't have team meetings during my class."

My behaviour reminded me of the Me I used to be. The one I didn't like much. The one who blamed other people for her unhappiness.

I didn't want to be that Me. That Me would be rude to the person I blamed for my discomfort, then feel bad, then try to apologize, then likely glare at an innocent bystander who happened to be close by. Then probably snap at one of my children.

Luckily, I recognize the warning signs now.
It's simple:
Anytime I don't feel great, I know there's a thought waiting to be replaced.

So during my lukewarm muscle workout, my brain worked overtime to find thoughts about this class that felt better.

It was hard for me, but I worked hard. And here's what I came up with:

"She's doing her best."

"This is the workout I was supposed to have today (because it's the workout I'm having, and I've never yet won an argument with reality)."

"I can still play full out."

"Yay me, for showing up here and not quitting."

At the end of the class, I politely thanked her, made a mental note of her name to avoid her classes in future, and went home feeling grateful for the opportunity to show myself that I really am the master of my experience, no matter what that experience may be.

The next day, would you believe, I was sore in places that haven't hurt in a while. And the good news is that it wasn't my head. And it wasn't my children's feelings.

Can you find the pause?

Between stimulus and response there is a space. In that space is our power to choose our response. In our response lies our growth and our freedom.
Rollo May, 1963

Can you find the space between stimulus and response?
It's important. Because this is what makes us human.
Remember Pavlov?
He convinced many psychologists that we go straight from stimulus to response.
As in

• see food ▶ salivate
• get yelled at ▶ yell back.

I'm convinced that between the stimulus and response, there is a THOUGHT about that stimulus, which creates a feeling, which determines our response.

As in
"I deserve a treat" ▶ feel self righteous ▶ salivate and eat it
OR
see food ▶ think, "I'm not hungry" ▶ feel neutral
(or, if you're me, proud) ▶ ignore the food.

As in
get yelled at ▶ think, "How dare she yell at me?" ▶ feel angry ▶ yell back
OR
get yelled at ▶ think, "This is all about her" ▶ feel detached ▶ walk away (or, if you're virtuous, give her a hug).

It seems that the same stimulus can produce many different responses depending on what we choose to think about it.

People ask me, "How do you change your thoughts in order to change your response?" Well, it's easy AND it's work.

Just as it took Pavlov many trials to condition the dogs to respond to his stimuli, we humans must take the time to train ourselves to find the space, dive into the space, eavesdrop on our thinking, choose the thought that will create the result we want, and condition ourselves to respond to that thought.

Even when the self-righteous thoughts, the angry thoughts, and the habitual thoughts pop up to compete.

There's the work.

Choose the thought that makes you feel better.

Choose the thought that promises you the result you want.

With practice, pausing into that space takes a split second.
No one will know but you.

It's the pause that makes you a leading actor in your life instead of a reactor.

It's the pause that takes us to a life consciously and mindfully lived.

Take that, Pavlov.

CHOOSE

Do you want to be exceptional?

Our common cultural belief is that some people are born exceptionally talented or smart - and some aren't - and these gifts allow those chosen few to excel.

I remember believing that.

Now, after years of working in different fields, with many varied professionals, I know it to be untrue.

My nephew, a serious, spiritual teenager, was discussing his future with me.

He was accepted into a prestigious academic program and received permission to defer his studies so that he could spend two years furthering his religious education.

He told me that he was considering changing his plans because he heard that this university program was rigorous, and he may not have time to devote to his religious studies, which are important to him.

"Of course you will," I told him.

He is one smart kid, my nephew.

You be another exception.

He thought I didn't understand, so he gave me examples of people he knew who had switched out because they couldn't do both.

"So what?" I said. "I know you can do it. Absolutely."

I could see a window in his mind opening.

"There was one guy who managed to do it all," he slowly remembered.

"Of course he did," I said.

"But he was the exception," he protested.

"So you be another exception."

"Be exceptional," I advised.

Then he said, "You can't choose to be exceptional."
And this blew me away.

I told my nephew there are many highly successful people who are not as clever as he is, and many unsuccessful people who have enormous talent.

We are all born magnificent, talented, smart, and capable.
What we do with our magnificence is up to us.

I hope my nephew chooses to stand high and be exceptional.

I hope he proves that it's entirely possible to excel at the toughest academic program while remaining a serious religious scholar.

I hope that he chooses to become the exception that younger religious boys talk about when considering their options.

I hope that you do too.

Be the exception.

Be the mom who parents with joy, while providing a magnificent income for her family.

Be the woman who loses weight, while eating with gusto and pleasure.

Be the person who stands up against prejudice, while remaining peaceful and loving.

Be the person other people look at and say, "If she can do it, maybe I can too."

Choose it.

Don't wait for it to choose you.

BE THE EXCEPTION

Trying will only get you more trying

How do you feel when you say "I'm going to try"?

If you pay attention, you may notice that this statement makes you feel weak, like you've given up before you've begun.

It sounds virtuous—it's as if you recognize that you want to improve and you are going to do your best. As if your heart is in the right place. But you know it isn't because of that weak feeling that you get. Feeling weak is always your clue that you're thinking something that won't get you what you want.

I recommend that if you want to change something, skip the word TRY and simply say, "I am going to do it." Here's why: we always prove our thoughts true. Whatever you say you are going to do, you will do that.

So if you're going to try to give up sugar, your result will be that you keep trying to give up sugar. You may give it up for a day or two. Then you'll feel tempted and you'll eat some. And then, you'll resist again, and on and on. Yep. You're trying, that's for sure. Problem is, you aren't succeeding.

You're never going to succeed until you DECIDE to succeed.
To DO it. Not simply to try to do it.

You don't have to change, but if you want to, then really commit.

Pick one thing at a time.

Understand that you can do whatever you believe you will do.

No exceptions.

And decide to do it.

If the best you can offer yourself is "I'll try," I recommend you skip that goal altogether because that tells me that you don't believe you will succeed.

And, in the same way that we will do whatever we truly believe we can, if we want to, the opposite is equally true—no matter how much we want to, we won't achieve it if we don't believe we can.

There's nothing more disheartening than really wanting it, trying, and failing, and not understanding that it was simply your thinking that caused the failure.

REALLY COMMIT.

You get what you work for

My youngest daughter is an excellent gymnast. I can't remember a time when she didn't spend almost every spare moment practicing and perfecting her skills and routines. She is completely self-motivated, determinedly persistent, and inspiringly thrilling to watch.

She does not get this from me.

People comment on how talented she is all the time. I suppose she must possess some innate talent, but this kid's accomplishments are a result of thousands of hours of repetition, review, more repetition, and more review.

When she was eight, she wanted to master pressing up into a handstand. She found a tutorial on YouTube and watched it daily for over a year. No one even knew about this until she asked me to spot her. She's still working on it, and she's almost got it. Three years on one move, and in the process, she's mastered many other difficult moves.

When she's not practicing gymnastics, she often hangs out with her mama. We bake, snuggle, read, talk nonstop, and get active together. It's always purposeful for her. When we jog, she gives me tips to improve my stride. When we swim laps, she teaches me how to get more power in my stroke. I don't even know where she learns it from, but I do know that she takes every suggestion from any coach seriously. And then she passes it on to me.

I invited her to do abs with me every night.
Because she is way ahead of me, with her rock hard little body, she gets to be the coach. After three of our proposed five sets of our first workout, I was dying. I thought it was perfectly acceptable to stop at three and build up slowly.
(Like I said, she doesn't get her determination from me.)
Not my daughter.
"Get up," she said flatly. "You don't get what you wish for.
You get what you work for."

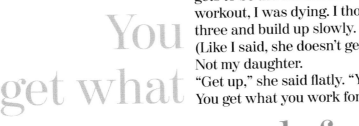

Seriously.

This from a ten-year-old.
Her room is filled with motivational sayings like this—all over her walls and even on her ceilings. She finds them or she makes them up.

So many of us adults talk about how one day we'll get in shape. We dream about it, plan for it, visualize it.
Wish for it.

And we don't get it.

My ten-year-old knows that the only way we're going to get in shape is if we get up from the dreamy couch, get onto our mat/treadmill/bike and do the work to get in shape.

Law of Attraction aside, my baby is here to tell you that, at least when it comes to our bodies (and maybe many more other things than I care to admit), you don't get what you wish for. You get what you work for.

What can you do if you really try?

I believe that all our actions stem from our thoughts, which is why it's important to pay close attention to what our mind is saying. This was demonstrated to me clearly one glorious spring day.

I'd been inconsistent in my exercise lately, and I was a few pounds heavier than usual. My mind decided this meant I must do gentle exercise. That I'm not fit enough to run, so I should power walk instead.

I like power walking, but running makes me feel fit and strong. Power walking doesn't.

That morning, I had invited my youngest daughter and son to join me on my power walk. We had a lovely walk in the ravine behind our home, climbed some steep hills, and then turned back. My baby loves to move fast, and about one kilometer from home, she said, "Let's run Mommy." We have a running routine—she moves like lightning and I do my slow jog, and she patiently waits for me at the end, coaching me on how to improve my stride.

Decide to be curious.

My first response was, "No, my love. I can't run this year." Then I heard myself, noticed how ridiculous and untrue that felt, and gave myself a slap on the head (gently).

I decided to be curious about what would happen if I ran, so I did.

Simply inviting in that curiosity resulted in me picking up my pace and running all the way home. Just because I was willing to try, I discovered that the only reason I couldn't run that year was my mind saying so.

I'm telling you this because it's a beautifully simple reminder that we shouldn't believe everything we think. Only those thoughts that feel good. Like,"I am still a runner," just because I say so.

How do you become a regular exerciser?

This may surprise you: it's all in the language you use. Your wording influences how you feel.

I recently spent a summer in Miami, and the first week, I started swimming 40 laps each day, while my kids played. I called it my 'Daily 40'. I didn't even think about my 'Daily 40' as exercise— my workout was my evening run on Bal Harbour boardwalk. It was just part of our daily Miami routine. I swam slowly, rested after every ten laps, and never really got breathless. Yet I quickly noticed how toned my arms and chest were becoming, which was amazing to me because it didn't feel like hard work.

But there it was, definite results.

I also noticed that I never missed a day. Even if we were out all day, I would dash down to make sure I got my 'Daily 40' in before the pool closed. When we came back to Toronto, I drove to friends' pools until they froze.

And my family always accommodated my 'Daily 40'.
Only because I called it that.
It was simply a reality.

I never consciously made a commitment to swim 40 laps every day. I believe that the reason it became a regular part of my day, without resolutions, struggle or will power, is because of the words I used to describe it to myself and to other people.

The Daily 40.
Kind of makes you think it's a daily occurrence, huh? Sort of like showering. Not something you really think about. Just happens because you think of it as a daily occurrence, so it is one.

DAILY

Got any stories that have outlived their 'best by' date?

Here's a story:

You: *Do you like your gym?*

Me: *The best part is that it's two minutes away. I can leave my house at 9:20 for a 9:30 class. If it was five minutes further, I just wouldn't get there.*

I believed this story, and it kept me at a gym I didn't enjoy for two years. I liked the classes, but not the environment. Much inner self-coaching occurred when I was supposed to be visualizing a tight butt. I believed it was true that I had exactly one hour and ten minutes for my workout. I repeated this so often that it became a fact in my mind.

For many years, I yearned to experiment with yoga as my daily practice, but there was no yoga studio within a five minute drive. Stuck in my story, I couldn't fulfill this desire.

Sometimes, all it takes is one simple comment to expose the lie in your story.

My sister told me that a new yoga studio had opened about 15 minutes from my house. I said, "It's too far" and she said, "It really isn't." That's all it took. She questioned my story and showed me it wasn't a fact—just a thought. And as she said it, I laughed at myself. I drive my daughter to gymnastics at that exact location, and I'm considering a karate dojo for my son right there, too. It takes a few minutes to drive there, and I never think about it.

The real truth is, like you, I'm completely in charge of what I do during the day. I get to decide whether driving 15 minutes to a workout that I love is worth it.

I decided to experiment and signed up for three months. I schedule the class I like best every day, and I plan my day around it.

Here's what I learned:

I get there most days.
It takes much more time than the gym.
I do have the extra time, if I choose to have it.
And I do.

Because being healthy and happy are necessary for me to do my work in the world. And because I'm worth it.
That's my story, and I'm keeping it.

You always get to decide how to react, and that always determines how you feel.

Most of the time, we think we're in a new situation, but really we're just repeating old experiences over and over because we let our brains think the same thing over and over. And of course, we end up with the same results. It's as if there's a little car in our brain and it keeps traveling down the same paths over and over.

The only way to change our result is by consciously choosing what to think about the situation. Imagine that the little car in your brain is at a fork in the path. Your car wants to go down the well-worn path, but you're the driver, and if you pay attention, you can turn the wheel and drive your car down a new path that will change your experience and your outcome.

But only if you're paying attention.

I went on an intense and inspiring women's trip a few years ago. On the last morning, we brought our bags to the lobby, colour-coded according to our final destination. My tags were yellow because I was taking the first bus to meet a friend.

After an emotional closing banquet, we arrived at 9:30 p.m., tired and ready for bed. Unfortunately, my suitcase didn't arrive with me. Dave, our bus leader, called the logistics coordinator to sort this out.

Trust that all would be well.

Initially, they doubted me—was I sure I'd used the right tag (yes)? Did I definitely put the bag in the right place (yes)? I noticed that my brain was offering me the choice to get irritated and I consciously said, "No thank you."

Then a woman wanted Dave's attention to discuss her shoes, which she'd left behind at the banquet. I noticed, again, that my brain offered me the choice to get indignant (doesn't she realize how trivial her problem is compared to mine?) and again, I consciously decided to reject the offer.

I patiently waited while Dave dealt with her, and decided to trust that all would be well, and that Dave was doing the best he could.

When my friend arrived, she didn't want to leave without my bag. I reassured her that it would all work out, and convinced her that we should go ahead with our fun night together.

I chose, consciously, to interpret this situation with acceptance and trust.

I was grateful for this trip. I was aware that it was unlikely that any of this was Dave's fault. I was sensitive to my tendency to blame the employee and knew that every time I did that, I felt sick after. Even if I apologized, that ashamed feeling never went away.

I planned that if my luggage didn't show up, I'd wash what I was wearing at my friend's house, and wear it on the plane. At home, I have more than enough of everything I need. My biggest concern was my laptop, and I realized that could be replaced in an hour.

I decided, with consciousness, to be calm and neutral about this. We gave Dave a ride home and he thanked me for being so nice about this. He told me that many participants had become more upset after losing a water bottle. Dave thought that it was because I was from South Africa, not America, but I know that wasn't true.

I've been that person that loses it over something small just because the organizer doesn't apologize as profusely as I expect — many many times.

It happens when I'm not paying attention to my brain. It happens when I let the habitual pathways in my brain take over my behaviour.

In the car, Dave received a text with a photo of my bag. When he showed it to me, I kissed his phone!! (Yes, I know. I'm embarrassingly passionate sometimes.) By the time we had dropped Dave at his home, my bag was already at the airport waiting for me, and we parted with a warm feeling about the whole event.

I was grateful that I hadn't lost it with him or the coordinator, and I didn't have to backtrack or apologize or feel that sick feeling in my stomach caused by shame and guilt.

My clients often ask me how to change habits that have been ingrained over many years.

IT'S WORTH IT

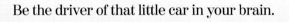

Here's how:

It takes consciousness.

It takes intentionality.

It's completely possible.

And it's worth it.

Be the driver of that little car in your brain.

"Did you know that believing on purpose is possible even when we are overwhelmed with grief?"

Of all the emotions human beings experience in a lifetime, grief is probably the most challenging. I choose to look at every challenge as an opportunity to grow. This doesn't mean I can always immediately pivot when I'm caught up in the turmoil of an emotional storm, especially when grief comes knocking on my door, nor do I always want to. But what I've learned about myself through my grieving is that no
matter how all-consuming my sadness feels, it has not actually consumed me. I am still me, underneath my sadness.

There were times in my life when that statement was the only thing I could hold on to, "I am still me underneath my sadness." It enabled me to endure my toughest grieving moments. It reminded me that I'm here for myself. Always.

I hope the following reflections will provide you with some comfort in difficult times. Find those beliefs that you know are true and hold onto them through your darkest moments. They will be your lifeline. And, above all, remember to be there for yourself.

I am still me underneath my sadness.

THINK DIFFERENTLY ——————

What to do with the pain?

Sadness. Loss. Fear. Regret. Worry. Crises rocking my world.

First, I slept. I ate. I hid. For two days.
It felt horrible.
Like I was congesting the pain, making it thick and doughy and sticky.
I felt thick and doughy and congested.

I wanted a different way. I knew a different way. Coached a different way. Taught a different way.
Feel the pain.
Accept the pain.
Allow it.

This wasn't your everyday twinge of sadness.
This was an all-consuming acute ache.
I could have cried or screamed at any time.
And still.
I let it be.
Let it in.
Let it do what it does.

Let
it be.

It felt real. Right. True. It felt like me, and I won't hide from me.
Because where would I go? And who would be there for me then?
It was an experiment. I could have gone back to sleeping, eating, and hiding. But I didn't.

So far, four noteworthy results from this experiment:

First: I didn't overeat.
I was an emotion-burying eater for many years. Yet, during an intensely painful time, I had no interest in extra food. Not an extra bite. It was easy to teach this when my world was solid. And it was the only thing to do when my world is spinning.

Second: I felt exquisitely alive.
I had moments of acute joy as well as sadness. I heard trees rustling all around the deck. I caught a glimpse of my husband's and daughter's heads touching as they collaborated on Sudoku. We all laughed during a family board game. All these moments had been experienced many times before. And the pleasure of them was magnified then because of the contrast.

Third: I held my life together.
I hosted 23 people for Mother's Day lunch. Taught a class on, would you believe, feeling our feelings. Coached, mothered, loved, wrote. I was a bit slower, a bit distracted at times, postponed some things that could wait, but I managed.

I was scared that if I let the pain in, it would overwhelm me, and I wouldn't be able to function. But that happened when I was hiding. My wise and perfectly tuned being knew when the pain can be at the forefront and when it should recede so I can manage my life. And when it interceded, I had a mantra: "I'm processing pain", and it strengthened me.

Fourth: I knew with certainty that this would end.
Not the situations—can't control that—but the pain.
My clients also fear that if they go in, they may never come out. But I saw it. A pinprick of light. I moved through it. Didn't know when or how—didn't need to.

And all of this surrounded by an enormous sense of wonder and gratitude:

"This that I teach and coach— it's real and it works."

You are loved

TRUST YOU ARE LOVED

My client was struggling with a major life-changing decision

Me too. Some uncertainty. I confronted something hard. I made a decision I wished I didn't have to make.

My client told me she wished she would get a sign from God that she was doing the right thing. She wanted a spiritual experience that would confirm what she knew to be true. She knew what it would feel like. She had experienced it before.

I told her that we don't get permission when we're adults. We make the decisions we make, and we get the good with the bad. Every time.

And yet I knew what she meant. We do get signs, messages, knowings. The thing is that we can't order them up. And when our head is full of chatter, worries, projections and self-abuse, it's hard to catch them.

While I was in a deeply relaxed state, these words, came into me:

"You will get through this."

"You must trust."

"You are loved."

I knew it was my mother, who I had lost the year before.
How did I know? I sensed her, unmistakably, and I felt immediate comfort.

Whenever my mind wants to go to worry again, I remind myself of these words, and that comfort is available to me instantly.

It doesn't matter how you interpret what I heard—depending on your beliefs, you could choose to see this as a message from God, an angel, random thoughts, or my mind making it all up. I like the idea that I am being taken care of by forces bigger than me that I can't see. And that my mother is looking out for me. My client feels comforted by the idea that God will guide her to the best decision for her.

I don't think we can depend on clear messages, though, because if we search too hard, we may miss the soft, subtle signs that are always there. What if we don't need to receive an explicit message?

I believe that these messages apply equally to all of us.
To my clients who are struggling, to you and to me.
You will get through this.
Trust.
You are loved.

You Can Be Sad and Amazing!

I discovered that I can be both sad and amazing. This was new for me. I had always focused exclusively on food as my self-medicator, and that blocked me from seeing that I also numb myself with other behaviours. I recently attended a week-long coaching program, and because I wasn't focused on my relationship with food, I got to explore what's been hiding underneath.

I learned that masking can be a medicator. I put on a mask to hide my true feelings? Totally missed this despite all the personal work I'd done. The thing that makes this tricky is that my mask felt real to me. My mask is called Amazing.

I really wanted to understand this idea. I usually felt amazing, and I had tools to feel better when I don't. I thought I was expected to be amazing and inspiring and happy. All the time.

And yet -
I've felt sad
and scared
and angry
sometimes.

As well as often amazing
and inspired
and happy.

So I realized that I can be both sad AND amazing at the same time.

It was a freeing concept. I didn't have to be happy and full of smiles in order to be the amazing person I was born as.
I just had to BE in order to be the amazing person I was born as.

Exactly as I am, at every moment. That is the amazing me.

So, yes, you can be sad and amazing, scared and amazing, happy and amazing, inspiring and amazing. All at the same time, or on different days.

And none of these mean anything about you, other than that you were born to feel the entire range of emotions available to us humans, without one making you more amazing than the other.

Which I personally consider to be a pretty amazing discovery.

AN AMAZING DISCOVERY

How are you feeling today?

Regret is never necessary.

I would usually visit my grandmother, Helen, on Saturdays. She lived alone and didn't go out. I do go out, and we loved to see each other, so I would go to her. We would sit together. I would bring a project I was working on, sometimes lunch, and we talked and talked and talked. She was the best at keeping secrets.
She was always my biggest fan.

Most Saturdays I loved going to see her. I looked forward to the haven of her quiet room, no interruptions, no demands, great conversation, mutual adoration, and sensible advice. But some Saturdays, I would look at my husband and say, "I don't feel like going today." He'd look at me sympathetically, and I'd say, "I'm off, bye." But some Saturdays, I didn't go—too busy, let time pass too quickly. Mostly I went and the visits fed me and her.

She died on a Monday.

So I couldn't go see her the next Saturday. I was free to do whatever I wanted that Saturday, and every Saturday to come.

When she died, my mind immediately went to regret:

"I should have gone more often."
"I should have called regularly."
"I should have visited her instead of going for coffee with my friend."
"I should have been there when she died."

I immediately recognized the futility of these thoughts, the drama they would create, and the absolute lack of any positive result.

So instead, I moved to gratitude

"I'm lucky to have had her for so long."
"I learned so much from her."
"She's finally at peace."
"I was able to help her."
"My husband and parents-in-law fed and cared for my children, so I could feed and care for my grandmother."
"The care at her senior's residence was compassionate, efficient, and family-centred."
"Her devoted caregivers were truly loving."
"My mother was with her when she passed."
"My sister-in-law's friend taught us how to give her permission to go."

So much to be grateful for.

And acceptance
"I did the best I could."
"This is exactly how it was supposed to happen."

I stopped being sad that I couldn't go anymore. I felt free and light.
And then I moved to promise. All the possibilities that this space
creates: cycling, tobogganing with my family, afternoon naps with my
husband, visiting people I don't see enough, playing board games with
my children, seeing what comes up.

Which brought me to
Freedom
and
Lightness

Sorrow may hit. A hole may appear. And I will let myself feel these
cleanly, all the way through.

And I know that if I do, they will take me all the way back to
Freedom
and
Lightness.

What void will you fill?

I was told that when someone dies, they leave a void. When each person who knew them takes a piece of the void, the hole gets filled.

When I lost my mother, I found this idea comforting. I felt my mother's presence acutely, even after. Her physical being had been powerful and spread enormous light on whomever she touched.

We were visited by hundreds of people the week after she died, and all shared similar stories—of immense kindnesses, of thoughtful gestures, of remembrances and follow-ups, of pain lessened when shared with her.

I decided what piece of the void I would pick up and try to fill – to increase my acts of kindness in the world. I started in an area where I'm usually not kind – I'm an impatient driver and don't like to be stuck behind a slow driver or wait for someone in front of me. I started slowing down, actively practicing kind driving.

I noticed two things:

1. My acts of kindness had a rippling effect: when I stopped and let a car in from a driveway or a parking lot, often the car behind me would stop after and let the next car in.

2. Being kind felt good to me. When I stopped to let a pedestrian cross the road where there was no crosswalk, I smiled, they smiled, we shared a wave, and I got a hit of warm and fuzzy. Not to mention a piece of my mom.

So I'm benefitting both in the knowledge that I'm helping fill the enormous void left by my mother's pure soul, and by receiving the gifts of connection with strangers. As a bonus, I get to enjoy the idea that my kindness is inspiring strangers to be kinder too.

I wonder whether you would consider performing an act of unusual kindness today, both to help fill the void left by my mother, a genuinely and selflessly kind and giving person, and to discover what changes for you when you do?

How to do Mother's Day without a Mother?

I wasn't sure who I would be on my first Mother's Day without a mother.

My mother being my mother was central to my existence.
This is how it is when you have a mother like mine: everything I did was inspiring and fantastic and gave her enormous joy. Every day. Unfailingly.

That Sunday morning, I came downstairs to a gourmet meal prepared by my husband and children.
The table was set with fancy china, napkins, and a cloth tablecloth. They up-leveled themselves by a thousand levels for me. We took pictures and had a bonded and appreciative meal together. Serious love bubble in the kitchen.

When I went to get dressed after, I suddenly felt like I'd been hit in the stomach. The first thing I would have done after breakfast would be to send my mom the photos of the feast with detailed descriptions and accolades. The last scone would have been packaged for her to taste. I knew this news would make her day. She would respond with a flowery message full of praise and adoration and gratitude. She'd let my husband and children know of her delight in what they did for me.

I think that's the reason I always took those photos.

Now what?

Even as an adult, my mother's enthusiastic pride and joy in me felt necessary.
Taken for granted until she passed.
Always always there.

Gone.

Suddenly and too soon.

And yet, still there.
I feel her so strongly at times it's almost as if she's more real now. Because she's inside me, and fills me, and sends me signs all the time. That she sees, that she loves, that she knows.

Grief is intense, yet merciful.
Mother's Day turned out to be peaceful and heart-warming.
Afternoon bike ride with my husband, silent hand holding at the lake, a bird chirping for our attention—my mother approving of our finding and giving comfort to each other. Evening hike with my family, sister, and nephew, gelato on an outside patio. We were careful with each other. Kind, gentle, appreciative of our fresh spring day.

I learned that I never know how I'll be. When I think I'll be okay, sometimes I can't hold myself together. When I'm scared I won't be able to be okay, like on Mother's Day, sometimes I'm happy.

I've learned that this is how to do life, grief included.
I just don't let story or expectation in. Whatever comes is allowed, felt, and then allowed to pass by me.

And always, always, overwhelming gratitude for a mother who insulated me in layers and layers of pride and praise and attention and love.

While she is physically gone,
her gift to me,
always available,
warms and sustains me.

What can you do if you can't make yourself feel better?

Angie, a woman I love dearly was badly burned.
She was sleeping and awoke, on fire.
The extent of her burns was serious.
Her partner died.
She is one of the strongest, bravest women I know. Tiny, gorgeous, energetic. She'd been the backbone of her entire family, who waited in her home country for the money she sent them every week and for her to bring them to live in Canada. Severe burns to her hands and arms may make it impossible for her to return to work.

I tried to find a thought that would make it feel, if not better, at least neutral. I couldn't. All I could feel was deep grief, sadness and loss for her, for her family, for her dream and for me.

And I decided, sometimes that's as good as it gets.
Sometimes, we just allow ourselves to feel our pain in a clean, deep way.

The discipline of thought work has taught me not to go to the "what if" or the "I wish" or the "why her?" or the "what will happen to?" thoughts because those will take me to a whole new level of panic and worry that will not help and will cloud my ability to see what I can do to help.

I chose to stay with the immediate grief in the present moment, every moment.

This way, my mind was clear to focus on what I needed to do without having to battle with the endless stories of unfairness or hardship that are part of our joint human programming and that do not benefit us at all.

I also knew that food wouldn't fix this.
In the past, when I received painful news, I was afraid of the intense emotion, and in order to avoid it, I would eat until I was numb.
But if I was numb, I couldn't help Angie. And thanks to years of thought work and choosing to live consciously, I was able to move through my day with this pit of grief and sadness.

Acknowledged it.

Explained to my kids why I was a bit distracted, without any blame.
Shared it, without sharing any interpretation of why it happened.
And I knew that my devastation would be there, until it wasn't.

I was available, being the person I wanted to be in this situation—accepting in an unacceptable situation.

Are you here? For you?

In her book *Daring Greatly*, Brené Brown teaches us that shame requires secrecy, and that way that we eliminate the shame is to speak our story to someone who will hear it with compassion. I like to think that person could be you, when you are able to retell your story in a way that generates self-compassion.

My advanced clients and I committed to a Six Month Challenge. We each chose an individual outcome, and worked towards our goals by studying our minds and learning how to use them to create what we want. It was enlightening, often fun and sometimes hard.

We spent a lot of time examining why we slide sometimes. You know how it is - you're in tune, connected, staying present, eating according to your body's desires, feeling on top of the world, and bam, you suddenly notice you've slidden into your personal hole.

Eating mindlessly, wearing sweats all day, pretending you haven't noticed. And, worst of all, you're engulfed in shame— you've been doing this work for a long time, you tell yourself you should know better, especially when you're a coach, as many of my clients are.

My Six-Month Challenge class decided that our private online forum would be our safe place to tell when we're sliding. Someone posted:

SLIDING

And the response, from another client, simply, "I'm here."

Even though I wasn't the one sliding at the time, I read this and felt immediately calm.

My nervous system downregulated "Aaaaaahhh."

Exhale.
Relief.
Thank you.

I'm HERE

So often, we worry we won't know what to say when someone is sliding. Or what to say to ourselves, when we're sliding. And no matter what's happening, all we ever need is to know that we are seen, heard, and met with compassion. And all it takes is, "I'm here."
No matter what you've done.
No matter what you've said.
No matter.
Whatever.

I'm here.

Conventional wisdom suggests that we need to hear this from someone else. I'm curious about whether we can do it for ourselves. I want that to be the case. No matter what. I'm here. For me.

In the past, when I would start to slide, my habitual tendency would be to pretend I didn't see it. It was as if I was in the periphery of my vision, struggling and numbing, and I determinedly kept my gaze straight ahead.

I decided to experiment with being here for me. I started to consciously turn my body around, so I was looking directly at the 'me' that I'm ignoring. And sometimes that's all it took.

That immediate calming of the nervous system.

The relief. Seen. Without judgment.

I'm here.

So be here.
For you.
And for your people.
No matter what.
And for you first. And always.

Has fear ever caused you to abandon your belief in yourself?

Fear prevents us from getting what we want out of life. Our fear leads us to create limiting labels that we live by without assessing or reflecting on their suitability for who we want to be.

Our deepest fears are often outdated because they originate in our primitive programming, which is no longer relevant. This is why, as we are about to embark on a new project, we're likely to feel intense fear that's out of proportion to the potential risks. This is because our primitive brain, which was designed to protect us from predators, believes that change is dangerous.

The problem is that our fear-filled brains haven't evolved to keep up with our current living conditions. Most of the time, when we examine our fears, we'll usually find that we are well able to withstand any of the consequences that may arise if our new project fails or we are rejected. More importantly, for those of us that yearn to keep growing and stretching and achieving, the potential benefit of that new project is going to far outweigh the potential risks, especially when you know how to use your wisdom to interpret any situation in your favour.

In this set of reflections, I recount moments where I embraced my fears and the lessons beyond the lessons that emerged as a result of these moments. I share these lessons with you as an invitation to embrace your own vulnerable and scary moments – the ones that challenge us to grow and find our deepest wisdom.

Every challenge is an opportunity to grow. It's in these moments of self-acceptance when we are able to move from being afraid to being fierce.

Every challenge is an opportunity to grow.

Is fear of failure stopping you? Just do it anyway

Our brains don't like change.
Our primitive brains continuously scan for danger—anything that is out of the ordinary smells like danger to them. They just don't understand it, which makes it seem scary.

But we humans—we also have highly evolved executive brains. And those parts of us yearn for growth, progress, and self-actualization. It's our evolved brain that guides us to start businesses that serve our community and the world. And it's our evolved brain that can calm us when we feel scared because our primitive brain is offering us scary thoughts. Our evolved brain just needs to understand that when we feel fear of failure or doubt, it means that we are doing work that matters.

To our family, customers, clients, patients, community.
To our soul.
To our world.

Fear is a tricky emotion.

There's intuitive fear that tells us we're in danger and we need to escape or change direction. We must get to know this type of fear and pay attention to it. It's usually quite prickly and wordless. It's pretty rare, though, as most of us reading this book are lucky to live in a safe and glorious world.

Then there's the fear that we create with our minds.
This fear is noisy. It tells us not to take action, not to evolve, to stay small, unseen. It tells us that it isn't safe to move forward or to put your magic out into the world.

"People will judge you."

"Your friends will abandon you if you're successful. If you fail. If you share your story. If you're too much of you."

The main reason entrepreneurs don't move forward with their businesses is that they haven't learned how to tell the difference between intuitive fear and fear created by their minds. They think fear of failure is an indication of danger and so they stop. They are paralyzing themselves with their minds.

When I tell my clients that their fear of failure, or Resistance, as Stephen Pressfield calls it, is a natural force that will always surface when they are stretching, they tentatively open up to the idea of moving forward, despite their fear. They just need to understand that this noisy fear is not their intuitive, guided fear. They engage their evolved higher brain and they are off to the races.

Think back on your deepest dream or your highest goal that you haven't yet achieved.

I ask you:

DO IT ANYWAY

What if when you feel fear about doing this, you do it anyway?

What would you do that you have not done?

What would you say that you have not said?

What would you publish that you have not published?

What would you achieve that you have not achieved?

All those answers—go do them.

Today.

Now.

Feel the fear and do it anyway.

That noisy fear—it's your sign that you're doing work that matters.

What's the difference between quitting and failing?

I always gave up when I wanted to avoid failing.

For me, that was often the first time something went wrong, or when things seemed too hard, or I didn't know what to do.

I thought I was going to fail, so I would just hit fast forward and quit. I never knew this about myself until I was clinging to a tree trunk in Tahoe. (You learn a lot about yourself when your lifeline is a rope connected to one Life Coach and a Master Coach is reading your mind as if it were an X-ray!)

Here's what I learned:

When I quit to avoid the possibility of failing, I am ensuring that I fail.

Let me back up a bit. Picture this: The Annual Life Coach School Certified Coaches Retreat in Lake Tahoe. A morning outing to Squaw Valley Adventure Center Ropes Course. This is not your average ropes course—I've done treetop trekking in the rain, without any problems. I don't scare easily. This course was different. We were told that it was designed to push your unique buttons. Their logo is "Altitude Adjustment"—a play on "Attitude Adjustment." A playground for discovering where your inner work is.

Before I began, my coach, Brooke Castillo, asked me how high I wanted to go.
I said, "I will go as high as I can."
"Are you sure?" she asked. If you knew Brooke, you would understand when I say I revised my goal to "I want to go further than I think I can." (Physically, I could go all the way.)

After about five minutes, the first time I wasn't sure where to put my foot, I said, "OK, I'm ready to come down now."

Brooke: "Really?"
Me: "Yes."
Brooke: "What are you thinking?"
Me: "I don't know what to do next."
Brooke: "What would you do if you did know?"
My resistance (aka my mind) stepped aside and I scampered up about two more feet.

"OK, I'm ready to come down now."
"What are you thinking?"
"This pole is in the way. I can't get past this pole."
(it intersected with the tree I was climbing).

50

How can you use the obstacle that's in your way?

"How can you use the obstacle that's in your way?"
Obviously.

The apparent obstacle was my support.
The pole was my next handhold.
It was my only way up.
It wasn't an obstacle at all, other than in my mind.

obstacle

"OK, I'm ready to come down now."
"What are you thinking?"
"This foothold isn't stable."
"Yep, sometimes it won't be completely safe," or, as Jessie, the cute owner of Altitude Adjustment (and honorary coach) put it:
"Sometimes this is as good as it gets."
Acceptance of what is.

Up I went.

And on and on we went.
I was shocked to learn how many times I was willing to quit when I could clearly go so much further.

Besides learning what a wimp I am, Brooke blew me away when she said, "Every time someone says, 'I'm done, I want to come down,' it's because they're afraid they're going to fall."

BUT coming down IS falling.

On this course, the only way down is to jump and then the belayer lets you down slowly—which is exactly what would happen if you fell. This is a great metaphor for me in my life as an entrepreneur, mother, wife, daughter, sister, and friend with many exciting ideas waiting to be birthed.

I decided right there that I was not going to do it anymore, and I haven't. If I fall now, it's because I fell trying. If I perceive an obstacle, I'll figure out how to use it to propel me forward. If I don't know what to do, I'll do what I would do if I did know. If I get scared, I'll remind myself of the unbeatable satisfaction I got from being willing to dangle midair and go beyond my mind's imagined limits. Knowing that the worst thing that can happen is that I'll learn a whole lot about myself on the way to where I'm going.

What are you dreaming of?

We took the kids to a dance performance with seven twenty-somethings, in peak physical condition, performing moves most people would think were impossible. They are only possible for them because they have chosen to live in bodies that are strong, supple and brave. This didn't happen by accident.

I've been coaching people of all shapes and sizes long enough to know that being in peak physical condition does not protect you from insecurity, shame, and self-hatred. These feelings come from what we tell ourselves about ourselves, and having a seemingly perfect body makes no difference to where our minds want to go sometimes. But I do know that there are many wonderful benefits to being in peak physical condition, and they go far beyond what you look like.

For me, these include:

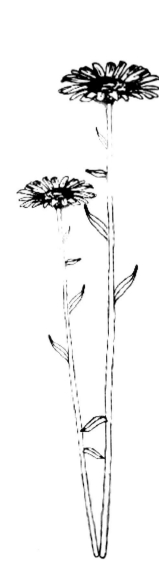

Being strong enough to do my own heavy lifting, instead of waiting for my husband to come home.

Knowing I can sprint to catch my flight if I need to (I always need to).

Joining my kids in any adventure that excites them, instead of sitting and watching from the sidelines like I used to.

Long, hard cycling dates with my husband and friends, instead of just meeting them for brunch after their ride like I used to.

Being able to exercise hard enough to use it as a stress releaser, instead of hiding in bed and eating.

So many of us use an event (wedding, vacation, reunion) or pick a date (New Year's day, birthday, tomorrow) to set ambitious fitness goals for ourselves. I want to offer this to you—the next time you set your goals, check in with yourself. The most important indicator of whether you'll achieve your goal is how you feel when you think about your goal.

Here's why:
If you don't feel good when you think about your goal, you're unlikely to achieve it. Even if you do, you won't sustain the results long term. This is because if you feel pessimistic about your goal, it means you don't believe you can do it. And our brain always sets out to seek or create evidence for what we believe. Every time you miss a workout, your brain will say, "See, I knew you couldn't do it," which will probably make you feel despondent and less likely to make that workout the next day. And then you tell yourself you've blown it—again.

THE FIRST STEP

If you want to make sure you achieve your goal, and I fully believe you can achieve anything you want, take the time, after setting your goal, to find out what you're really thinking about it. Clean up your thinking that is creating doubt in your ability to achieve it, and lastly, state your goal in a way that feels believable to you. This can be challenging, especially if you have a history of giving up on yourself and your dreams.

SET YOUR GOAL

CLEAN UP YOUR THINKING

STATE YOUR GOAL

CHANGE YOUR BELIEFS

How will I know when it's time to quit?

Perfect biking weather makes me feel inspired to create.

I put my laptop in my backpack and set off on my first ride of the season down through the ravine to my favourite coffee shop for salad and sacred writing time. My chosen route had a long steep hill at the end. The last time I biked up that hill, I did it with great ease, but I was fitter and lighter than I am now. I became nervous as I approached the hill because I was already thinking that I couldn't do it this time. I told myself I would try. That riding some of the way is better than nothing, that I can always get off and walk if I need to.

Wow. Even before I started up, I was already giving myself permission to quit. Long before I started to struggle. And I know that if my thinking goes to quitting, my actions are going to follow.

Luckily, I'd been reading *You Can If You Think You Can*, and had just finished the chapter titled "It's Always Too Soon to Quit." About a quarter of the way up the hill, it pinged in my head. "It's always too soon to quit." And I held that thought in my mind all the way up. I completely adjusted my thinking. I reminded myself that I could downshift as much as I needed to make it up that hill. I found another option because suddenly the action of quitting was no longer available to me. I had removed it with my mind.

I made it up the hill. Of course I did. On the eighth gear—I had four downshift options left that I didn't use. No surprise. It was hard. Much harder than the last time. My heart was pounding and I was breathless. My usual habit would have been to quit long before I got this tired.

Think about the shifts that holding this thought—"It's always too soon to quit"—would have on people who are building a business.

Some think that every moment is the right time to quit.
The minute they miss one podcast. Or a client asks for a refund. Or no one signs up for their webinar. Or they miss their monthly target. I remember when I thought that way. I invite them (and you) to consider this idea: If you really want something, whatever it is, then it's ALWAYS too soon to quit.

Suddenly, other options become available: Get up early and record the podcast tomorrow. Offer the refund from abundance and double your offers to fill the spot. Record the webinar and post it on social media anyway. Maybe it's time to consider marketing a different way. All ideas they would have missed if they had thought that 'hard' signalled quitting time.

Think about it for a moment—if it was too early to quit, what would you keep doing, and how would it feel when you got there?

Where have my genius skills gone?

I was wobbling in yoga.
Seriously.
On one foot.

WHAT?
This was supposed to be easy for me!
I'm a yogini.
I was born a yogini.
And from someone who's been terrible at every sport since birth, discovering that I was naturally good at yoga was quite a revelation!

Yet there I was in hot yoga struggling to regain my composure during tree pose. (Trust me, it's hard to look composed when you're sweating all over the floor even when you're not wobbling.)

I had introduced a new variable into my yoga practice - heat. My body had been craving warmth, and I was thrilled to discover hot yoga — instant addiction.

I ditched zumba, body pump, kickboxing—and dreamed all day about the warm room, the poses, the stre-e-e-etching, the quiet.

My poses are deeper, and they feel effortless.
Except.
I can't balance on one leg.
But I CAN. I always can.
For ages.
Gracefully and perfectly aligned.
But not here.

Approach your struggle with fascination.

Sometimes if my mind's not balanced, it's reflected in my poses.
But this is every class. No matter how hard I tried. Or which way I tried —
Focus
Squeeze
Let go
I wobbled and fell over while everyone else in the class was still.

I decided to approach this with fascination - I was always quick to give up as soon as a physical activity became challenging. But I have decided to remain committed to my yoga practice and the fascination of what there is to learn about myself and my mind.

I'm excited about this.

I love it too much to quit even though I'm not brilliant at it.
This is new for me. I usually only do things I'm brilliant at (which has led to a high achieving, but narrow resume).

So the way for me to do this is to undergo an identity change.
I am morphing from 'Bev the Quitter' to 'Bev the Stayer.'
Not sure yet exactly how you do this thing called persevering.
Fortunately, I have experience with mastering the poses. Still, I have no experience with staying with something when it's hard.

But Eagle Pose, Tree Pose, Dancer Pose
(man! my used-to-be-best show-off pose!)...
I have a hunch they'll teach me. I believe they've been created for this purpose. And I'm looking forward to experiencing the thrill of mastering a skill which did not come naturally to me.

Soon you'll see me in Dancer Pose - standing solid in my own sea of sweat (and hopefully no tears)!

What would you do if no one was watching?

I broke a personal barrier.

I danced while no one else was dancing.
Almost. I danced with two friends at a party of about 40 people.

Before then, I was a person who only danced when everyone was dancing.
I was always mesmerized by women who got up and danced at concerts or parties without making sure that other people were dancing before.
I was awed and delighted by them.
I was tempted to join them.
But my belief that I couldn't separated me from them and the possibility of this joy.

I was at my friend Julie's 40th birthday party marvelling at another effervescent friend, Deb, dancing up and down the garden all on her own. I watched her and thought, "One day I am going to do that."

As I was saying good-bye to Julie, Deb ran up to invite her to come and dance. I said, "Good for you guys, one day I will do that too." And then I heard myself say to myself, "Or this day?" Instant excitement.

I told Deb I was about to break a personal barrier, and she gave me the key:

"Dance like no one is watching."

Really? I could do that?

Dance like no one is watching?

But they're all there.

That was the worry behind my barrier.
I thought they would all be watching. And judging. Negatively.

What if no one was watching?

Well then. DANCE baby!!!!
And we did.
For hours.
Three of us.
Laughing.
Shimmying.
Singing.
Sweating.

NOT ONE DROP!

P.S. No alcohol.

Not one drop.

And who knows if they
watched or didn't.

I was having way
too much fun to care.

I don't have to protect myself from people!

I had the pleasure of taking my daughter out for lunch to celebrate her birthday. Seated next to us, a group of politicians were planning their strategy for our upcoming election. I shared my strong political opinions with my daughter, who told me I should get involved.

We both laughed at the idea. "Oh, that's right," she said, "you don't like people."

It's a running joke in our family that "Mommy doesn't like people."

We used it as an excuse for many things, which is funny, because I love lots of people, and my life's work is all about people. But I kept this self-imposed label as a protection against unwanted interactions and I became curious about why I created this.

I started noticing how many times I raise my 'shield' in public, as if I need to protect myself from 'people.' I've been fortunate to live in a safe place, so it's not physical protection. What was it then?

I had recently learned that Empathy is one of my top five strengths (*Clifton Strengthsfinder*) and I think that my 'people-avoiding persona' was a misguided attempt to protect my heart from too much caring.

Maybe, but there must be a better way—what if I could love people and not get bogged down in empathy?

I decided to try one while walking to my gate for my flight home from a workshop. The couple in front of me on the jet-bridge were people I would have judged and made sure to avoid eye contact with in the past (I won't go into details of how I judge because that's not interesting at all, being completely random and unproven). She was joking to him about the long hallway and how fancy it was and how important she felt. Next thing, she turned around and brought me into the fun.

For the first time, I just hammed it up with her.

"Right!!! Except the carpet should be red. And there should be cameras popping." And then she pretended to pose and wave them away. And we laughed. And then they sat down in their seats, we said, "Have a good flight," shared one more smile, and I went on to my seat.

This may not seem like a big deal to you at all because you're probably a nice person who likes people. But honestly, for me, it was quite freeing. I engaged, had fun, even looked them in the eye, and they didn't need a thing from me.

It took nothing away from my heart. In fact, it filled my heart a bit because it was fun and warm and sort-of-but-not-really funny. How often do we create labels and assertions about ourselves that cause us to develop behaviour patterns that aren't us in our best light, without ever assessing or reflecting on them?

As a child growing up in apartheid South Africa, I was acutely aware of all the pain and suffering. I thought I needed to harden myself against people and avoid engaging as much as possible, in order to save myself from their suffering. I didn't know then that my suffering was caused by my thoughts. It's not even caused by my own situation, never mind someone else's.

Now I go about my day wondering—what if it's possible to open my heart and know that I can take care of my heart at the same time? I'm having so much more fun, and I am happy to report that the answer is yes.

This is what it's like inside my head, my friend.

A simple comment from my lovely daughter takes me on a whole journey down the craziness in my mind. So glad you're here to share it with me.

TAKE CARE OF MY HEART

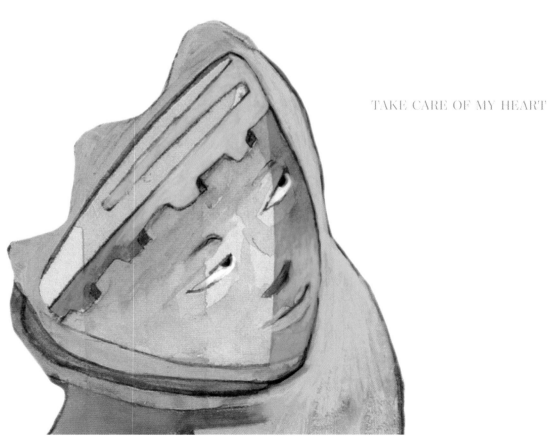

What to do when you're having a meltdown?

I had a minor meltdown one Thursday night.

We'd invited guests for dinner on Friday night. The house was a disaster, and I had decided that my Friday was overly scheduled. While my husband was tidying the house and planning what he would buy for dinner the next night, my youngest daughter was baking brownies, and my oldest daughter was preparing to bake cookies (dessert definitely takes centre stage when we entertain!), I was complaining about how unfair it was that all the responsibility for cooking fell on me (while doing little of anything).

My husband gave me a hug. He didn't say a word.
I dissolved into tears crying about all the things I had to do every time we had guests (none of which I was doing while everyone else was preparing).

You would have been forgiven for thinking I was a three-year-old in a fifty-year-old body.

My husband stood behind me with his hands on my shoulders.

He didn't say a word.
He didn't even move.
He stayed with me.
And I felt it.
I felt his 'being with me' no matter what.

No judgment. Full compassion. No opinion about my tirade.
Best of all, no belief that he should do anything to make me feel better.
This was the crux of it for me.
His doing nothing to make me feel better made me feel better.

He taught me that I don't need anything outside of myself to feel better. That nothing outside of me can make me feel better. That my pity party was a choice. And that ending the party was my choice.

After a few minutes, I stood up, announced to the family that I was done, and then we all got to work.
There was no emotional residue.

I loved how it went. The whole sequence.
My husband and I have done many different dances around this.
Me complaining, him defending. Me complaining, him fixing. Me complaining, him hiding. All of these ended in disaster.

This one. Him staying. Just staying. In love and acceptance.

That's the one.

Which got me thinking...

What if I could do that for myself?

When I'm having a thought storm?

Instead of yelling at someone or eating a bag of cookies, what if I could just sit with myself? Metaphorical hand on my shoulder. Letting me know I'm there. No attempt to change or be different. No need to explain or fix or change myself. Just be. With me.

Just thinking about it brings me such a feeling of relief.

You?

Let's share our shame to release it

"Shame cannot survive being spoken...It cannot survive empathy."

—Brené Brown

I had a magical week where I felt more alive and in touch than I had felt in ages. I know why. I spoke my shame – to my friends and to my blog readers (I used to write a weekly blog called 'Your THIN is in your THINKING'), and they met me with empathy, support, and love. I received many emails and texts from my readers, who wanted to let me know that they are here for me, no matter what. And with each message I received, I felt lighter and brighter.

I didn't notice it at first. I just noticed that I went to sleep at a normal hour that week (no Netflix). I woke up every day feeling energetic. I worked out every day, I followed my schedule, and I ate only the fuel my body required. These are my barometers for how I'm doing, and I'd been failing at most for many weeks before that. I didn't struggle to be different that week. It just happened naturally.

And I realized why—

I spoke my shame.

And it was met with empathy.

It's gone. It's exactly as Brené Brown says:

"Shame depends on me buying into the belief that I'm alone."

My readers showed me I wasn't alone, and now it's gone.

In addition to the support, I also received emails from my readers telling me about their shame and how much it weighs on them. One dear soul sent me this subject line, "My shame weighs 80 lbs."

Dear reader. Don't. You don't need to.

Whatever you have done,

Whatever was done to you,

You don't need to hide it.

And you are not alone.

YOU ARE NOT ALONE

Who knew wobbling could feel so POWERFUL?

I made an amazing discovery. There are many many steps and adjustments between failing and mastery. It happened during hot yoga, my incubator for spiritual and physical development, while I was attempting my favourite pose. You guessed it...

Tree pose. Again.
I was doing my usual.
Focusing.
Trying not to fall.
Staring hard at my water bottle.
Sweating.
Not zen.

As I stumbled, I looked to my yoga teacher for inspiration expecting to see her in perfect tree pose, a model of harmony.
Instead, she was wobbling.
Hopping around on one foot actually. Intent on returning to her pose.

I looked around. Many of the students were not perfectly still. They were continuously making adjustments in order to maintain or improve their pose. They weren't giving up the minute they lost their balance.

There are many steps between falling and mastery.

Fascinated and excited, I decided to play a bit. I found my pose, which I could usually hold for a few seconds. Then, when I started to lose my balance, I decided to do everything I could not to put my foot down. I contracted my core and supporting leg. Stayed with the wobble. That worked for a bit.
Next, I tried tiny hops around the mat until I found stillness, putting my arms out to my sides if necessary.

Eagle pose was next. I squeezed all my limbs even more tightly into each other when I started to wobble. Different wobbles for different poses.

Would you believe, almost every time, every balancing pose, I succeeded in regaining my balance? I never believed it was possible. So I never tried. Honestly.

Most people I've told about this laugh at me. "Of course you struggle and experiment and try different things, if you really want it."

I never knew. For me, if I wanted it, I tried it. If I didn't get it quickly, I moved on to wanting something else. I've been fairly good at getting some things I want. But the one thing I never got good at is wobbling (unless you count my thighs).

I never developed resilience. Never experienced the huge thrill of mastering something that was not naturally easy for me. My childhood was littered with castoffs from activities tried and dropped after a few weeks—tennis rackets, ballet shoes, geometry sets.

In adulthood, if a job became challenging or boring, I just switched jobs or careers, without a second thought. It never occurred to me to stay, wobble a bit, and find a new level of mastery.

I always felt pity for people who struggled with things. Lately, I've admired them. I've been fascinated with them. I've been following them around, quizzing them on what they're thinking, asking why they don't just give up. These people—it doesn't occur to them to quit. Because they don't expect automatic mastery.

I improved my balance poses practicing in this new environment. They weren't pretty, not always still and strong. But I didn't give up on them, and I'm way closer to success than when I simply put my foot down at the first wobble and gave up until the next class.

And I put out an energetic call for off-mat wobbling opportunities. That night, my daughters invited me to play Dance Dance Revolution with them. I am the world's worst dancer. But you know what? I fumbled through it, had fun with them, earned a few C's among my FAIL's, and hopefully taught them something I never knew until recently: staying with hard things can feel empowering.

Have you ever been willing to acknowledge how uniquely magnificent you are?

We all need a reminder to be who we are.

We get lost listening to that other voice inside – the nasty critic – who is also us. It haunts us when we try to do something big or something new. When we decide to chase our dreams, that other voice asks, "Who do you think you are?" It tells us we don't deserve to have what we want. It can be harsh and undermine all the positive strides we take. When we try to ignore that nasty inner critic and shove down those negative feelings, we lose access to who we truly are.

True You—that voice that expresses your deepest wisdom— never indulges in lies such as "I don't know why...," "It's not my fault," or "I can't do it because..." Even though it's tempting to pretend, True You knows how to grow in order to create the life you want. Moreover, True You is certain that you already have everything inside you to do the work and succeed beyond your dreams. When we let go of these lies we make way for a clear path to "I do know," "I choose to take responsibility for...," and "I can do it."

Get to know how True You feels, acts, and thinks. It's worth spending time on this because the more familiar you are with True You, the more likely you are to recognize when you are operating from that nasty critic, or the excuse-maker. Step back, dive into your deep wisdom, and reinhabit your True You, which is where all your magic lies.

We all need a reminder to be who we are.

The following reflections encourage you to come out of the dark and stop hiding your true self from yourself and others.

What does it cost you to not be yourself?

Most of us can remember a situation where we did not speak our truth because we were afraid of hurting someone's feelings.
Annie said yes to a lunch date she didn't want to accept.
Mary made a promise she doesn't want to keep.
I offered to refer clients to a practitioner I don't want to refer to.

Why do we do it?

We think it's being some version of 'not nice' if we don't.
Growing up, we were taught to be nice, and not to hurt other people's feelings.

Here's what I want to teach you.
You can't hurt other people's feelings.
That is their privilege and theirs alone.

Hear me on this one: NOTHING you do can hurt someone's feelings.
You can try to hurt their feelings and you can intend to, but you have no power over whether you succeed or not.

And the opposite is also true.
You can want to avoid hurting their feelings, and you can try to do what you think will achieve this goal, but you have no power over whether you succeed or not.

How do I know this?
Because our feelings are a direct result of our thoughts.

Try this.
Think of someone you love a lot.

How do you feel now? I'm guessing warm and fuzzy.
Now think of someone who irritates you.
You feeling it?

See—you just switched your feelings without those two people having to do anything at all.
You caused yourself to feel pain, and you caused yourself to feel love.
You're the only one who can cause yourself to feel any and every emotion.

You may want to argue with me and say that the only reason you feel love is that that person is loving towards you.
I understand. It makes sense to you to love them, so you do.
But what I want to show you is the reason it makes sense to you is that you think that they are a lovable person.

It's possible because that person you love is irritating to someone else because they don't think that those qualities you love are lovable at all.

BE YOURSELF

Here's how I know it's true.
Think about your 'Lovable Person'.
Does everyone in the entire world love her in the same way you do?
Or even everyone who knows her?
I'm guessing not.
We all elicit different emotions from different people.
Why is that?

If your feelings for me were a result of how I behave, then everyone would have the exact same feeling about me because I'm the constant.

So what's the variable?
Our thoughts (perspectives, interpretations, judgements),
based on our programming and experiences.

You with me?
Okay.
So then.
If you say "no" to lunch because you don't want to go, some people will have hurt feelings and others won't.
I personally would prefer it. I will have grateful feelings.
I don't want you to pretend to be my friend—I would actually find that quite hurtful.
So, if she did feel hurt because you told her you didn't want to do lunch, it wouldn't be because of what you said.
It would be because of what she thought to herself about what you said:

"She doesn't like me. I'm not likeable. I'm a loser. No one wants to hang out with me."

If I didn't feel hurt, it would be because I'm thinking,

"We're not meant to be friends. Sometimes that's what happens. Good to know."

When you're deciding whether to do something you don't want to do for fear of hurting someone's feelings, remember this -
You can't hurt anyone's feelings without their consent.

Now, they may not know this, and they may think you hurt their feelings, but truly, the only person who can hurt their feelings is themselves, with the interpretation they choose to give your refusal.

So...what else would you rather be doing?
What joy, what authentic friendship will you create?
What promises will you make wholeheartedly and with great conviction?

I promise you that if you decide to focus on your feelings and not hurting yourself with your thoughts, you will unburden yourself of complication and worry about something that is out of your control.
Now there's a promise I can make with wholehearted conviction.

YOU must believe you are lovable before you can believe someone else loves you

Jane wants her father to tell her she's smart, lovable, and accomplished. Many coaches might help her figure out how to tell her dad what she wants from him.
Not me.
And here's why.

Whenever we think we want someone else to tell us something about ourselves, it means we're desperate to hear it from ourselves. Jane didn't believe me. But when I asked her if she thinks she's smart?
Lovable?
Accomplished?
She became flustered and started to stammer.
She couldn't answer me.
She tried to talk herself into thinking she's smart, tried to find evidence for it. But she couldn't—she didn't believe it herself.
She wants to believe she's smart and lovable and accomplished, but she doesn't.

And she thinks that if her father tells her she's smart, it will make her believe it.

It will make her feel better.

Never works.

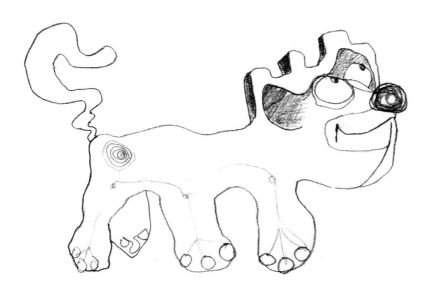

Here's why:
It won't land unless she believes it.
I grow vegetables in my front yard every summer.
Lush arugula bushes and overflowing tomato bushes.
One year, I tried to plant in my shady backyard and I got nothing.
The seeds and plants were the same, but the conditions in which I planted them were different.

Think of Jane's mind as the soil.
Let's say she doesn't believe she is smart or lovable.
Her soil is barren and there's no sunlight.
Let's say her dad praises her all day and all night.
It's like planting seeds in barren, shady soil. No matter what you do, they won't grow.
Those compliments won't take hold.
They'll have no effect.

Jane starts to think it's the seeds—if only someone would give her better seeds or their seeds, then it will work and she'll feel better. But all Jane needs to do is work on the soil—her soil, which is her mind—and then she won't need to change her seeds or get anyone else's. When her soil is fertile, her plants will grow.

If you believe you are unlovable, stupid, or worthless, I can tell you the opposite a thousand times a day, and you won't believe me. You won't feel what you think you'll feel when I tell you. Just like I can sprinkle seeds on barren soil all day and nothing will grow.

So........instead of Jane trying to get her father to change, which will take effort and is unlikely to work, she can just take a shortcut.

All she needs to do (all you need to do) is:

* Figure out why YOU don't tell yourself how lovable, smart, and accomplished you are.

* Figure out how all your objections are untrue.

* Figure out how to find it in you all by yourself.

Because if your dad, or anyone else, compliments you and your soil is barren, then it won't land or make you feel better.
And if they compliment you and you already believe it, your soil is fertile. There's already a beautiful garden and their compliments may just lead to an extra few tomatoes. Or not.

Because you can grow those extra tomatoes yourself.

So much easier, right?

Does it matter what other people think?

We spend so much time worrying about what other people think about us without ever questioning whether it matters.

One night, I arrived at an event with my family, all dressed up and fancy in my fitted little black dress (feeling quite hot, if the truth be told).

The room was crowded and we had to walk across the front of the room to the open seats.
When I sat down, my mind started to spin. All on it's own.
"Was my stomach sticking out?"
"Could you see my pantyhose line?"
"I should have sucked my stomach in."
Tiny, barely audible voices that I almost didn't hear.

I tuned into them because I felt a mild tightness in my head.
That's my clue that my mind has started to play an ancient, well-worn recording that no longer serves me.
And if I don't tune in, it will replay endlessly until I'm exhausted or snap at whoever is near me, or overeat.

So I pay close attention to my bodily sensations.
Soft and still tells me my mind is clear and often empty.
Tightness is always my sign that my mind needs some attention.

I listened in to the voices.
For a few moments I actually believed them, which led me to think that this was a real problem.

Until a soft, certain voice inside me said "it doesn't matter," and I instantly softened.

My body relaxed and I immediately saw the truth of this:
It didn't matter at all if my stomach was sticking out and everyone saw, or my pantyhose line was pinching my waist and everyone saw.
Nothing in my life would change if they did.

Not one thing.

I recognized this to be true with absolute clarity.
And it changed my entire experience of that event.
I relaxed into my chair, turned to play with my daughter's hair, and swam in the stillness of the moment.

Every time I ask a client "So what if they saw/knew?" they stop, think, and eventually say,
 "So nothing."

I'm still me.

Sometimes they'll try to convince me about all the implications, but if I keep asking "so what?", eventually, we always get to the same place.

It doesn't matter.

I'm still me.

Here.

Present.

Alive.

Choosing how I experience this moment.

Can you nudge against the sound of your own

One of my inspiring teachers asked this question during class one day.
She was referring to the sound of the mesmerizing band that accompanies our Nia dance.
What a great question, I thought, thinking of my thoughts.
Can you nudge against the sound of your own thoughts?
Can you get a little closer and listen in to what you tell yourself?

"I'm stressed because my son can't cope at university."

"I overeat because my husband is never home."

"I don't have enough time."

"My daughter is driving me crazy."

"I'll never make enough money."

"I'm out of control."

My clients think these thoughts all day, every day.
This is a sample from just one group coaching session.
I felt exhausted and drained just typing them.

Listen

Your freedom depends on it.

My fingers literally felt heavy.
We don't even notice this constant chatter.
We are so used to the internal whipping.
I asked my group to repeat these thoughts to a picture of themselves as a small child. Not one of them could do it.
Yet we talk to ourselves this way all day every day.

Can you nudge in and listen?
Your freedom depends on it.
Those treacherous thoughts?
They're the cause of your overeating, overspending, oversleeping, over-anything.

Can you nudge in long enough to take notice?
Your freedom depends on it.
Grab them.
Bring them to your consciousness.
You can change the thoughts.
It will change how you feel.
Then you will change how you behave.
And your life's results will be different.

Nudge against the thoughts.
Stay with yourself as you pull them out of the darkness.
Don't be afraid as you feel the feelings.
Breathe with you as you find the replacement thought that brings you peace.
How will you know it? It's a thought you believe with certainty.
And it makes you feel better.
Hear yourself sigh with relief and see your body relax and smile.
You'll enjoy nudging against your calming, joyful thoughts.

At the end of the group, my clients believed that:

"My son's studies are his business."

"My husband is a good man."

"I have the exact amount of time I need."

"That's just my daughter being my daughter."

"Maybe money is possible for me."

"I am learning that I choose to be in or out of control."

Better thoughts to nudge against for sure.
Not free and clear yet.
But better.
And a thought that is just a bit better to nudge against
feels a lot better to feel.

Don't make grandiose promises to yourself
(unless you've kept them before)

I don't advise that you promise "to give up sugar forever," or "to work out every single day," or "to be early for every appointment for this entire year". I heard these commitments from my clients over the course of one week.

Here's why I discourage promises like this, even though I know that if you stick to them, you will achieve your goal:
Promises like these don't usually feel very good to us.
And we don't usually do something (for long) if it doesn't feel good.

When I asked my clients how they felt when they thought about these promises, they said:

"Tight."
"Excited, but nervous."
"Defeated."
"Angry."

When we explored the reasons for these feelings, we discovered these beliefs:

"I won't stick to it."
"I should have done this long ago."
"It will be impossible for me."
"I've failed before."

With underlying beliefs like these, it's highly unlikely that they will keep their promises, because we usually create what we believe we will create, which is failure in every example here.

The problem with these grandiose promises is that they embody 'black and white thinking', or 'perfection thinking'.

"'So?" You may be thinking, "We all want to be perfect."
Wanting to be perfect sounds helpful, but here's the problem with wanting to be perfect: the minute you break your promise—the minute you eat sugar, or skip a workout, or arrive late—you tell yourself you're imperfect, you've blown it, and you give up completely.

Until the next grandiose promise—that lasts a day, a week, or a month.

I'm going to take a guess that you've tried this before and failed.
So you won't believe yourself the next time you try it.

How about aiming smaller and building up some evidence for yourself that you can and do keep promises to yourself?

Here's how:
Add one word to your promise: Today.
Today, I won't eat sugar.
Today, I'll work out.
Today, I'll stick to my diet.
Aaah.

Immediate relief.
Certainty.
Calm.
Lightness.

Jody said, "One day at a time is manageable. I like the idea of renewing my commitment each day because usually, once I've kept my commitment for a few days, I move onto something else or forget and then I'm back where I started. Making a conscious decision each day feels do-able and track-able."

Make one
promise
to
yourself.

Try it.
Make one promise to yourself for today.
Then tomorrow, you get to choose whether you want to make it for today again.

And the next day.
And every day that you keep your promise to yourself, you're building trust that you are dependable and you do what you say you'll do.

So, when you make that promise the next day, you will feel certain and calm, which produces much more effective results than tight and nervous.

Some days are tough, and that's okay

I had a great day planned— a morning of work I love, a shopping date with my daughter and a friend to buy decor for her newly renovated room followed by lunch together, then dress shopping with another daughter, and ending with dinner at a friend's pool. It should have been a winner all round.

But at some point in the day, I started to feel disgruntled and dissatisfied, and then, surprise, I felt the urge to eat.

I don't eat in between meals—it's a commitment I made to myself a long time ago and I'm focused on becoming a person who keeps my commitments to myself.

So instead, I watch myself crave.

I let whatever thoughts want to float into consciousness be there along with whatever emotions and sensations arise in my body.

Most of the time, being with myself is an okay place to be. But not that day—that day there weren't any words—there was just disgruntled. Dull.

And you know what? I can handle that.

I can handle whatever I bring myself on any day.

I know I won't eat, even though a part of me wants to.

But the deep, wise part of me, that's in charge as long as I stay present, knows that my deepest desire is to be a person who keeps her promises to herself.

It's a beautiful thing to know that you can be with yourself no matter what.

You may think this is too hard for you because your thoughts are too ugly and your feelings too hateful.

And it may hurt.

NO MATTER WHAT

Staying present you get all of it.

But here's what happens: when you commit to staying with yourself, which means you don't distract yourself with food or Facebook, you start to notice that your thoughts come and go, even the hateful ones, and that in between is peace, or silence, or a smile.

If you'd distracted yourself the minute you wanted to numb the hateful, you would have missed that smile.

Staying present—you get all of it.

Numb with food or Facebook—you rob yourself of all of it.

I know which I'm choosing—you?

How do you feel when you make an excuse?

Excuses are tricky because, while they do provide relief from having to take responsibility in the moment, if you dive into your own wisdom, you will probably find that they don't sit well with you.

Even if you were let off the hook, the ultimate feeling of weakness and shame isn't worth it.

What do you make excuses about?
Two common topics are:

What we eat
(I couldn't help it. I was starving and there was nothing healthy to eat),

How we feel
(He was rude. I just had to yell at him),

We often believe our excuses.

But they never bring us true relief. If I ask my clients how they feel when they say something like this, they usually shrink, and tell me they feel weak, embarassed, or stupid.

That's how I know excuses are a lie.

Whenever you think something that makes you feel bad, I assure you that it's not true, and it definitely will prevent you from reaching your goals in life.

I believe that we are all born innately peaceful and joyful.
So if this is our natural state, then anything we think that causes us to move out of this natural state is untrue.

Let's look at two of these examples:

"I couldn't help it. I was starving and there was nothing healthy to eat."

You can always help it. As an adult in a free world, you can always arrange to have healthy food with you or to go out and get it.
I can think of maybe ten scenarios where this may not be possible, like on a freeway at midnight.
Still, you could have packed food for the long drive, right?

"He was rude. I just had to yell at him."

Own your emotional world.

You know those people who don't yell back when someone yells at them?
They are the powerful ones.
They know that no one can make them feel anything or make them do anything.
They're in charge of their emotions.

You can be too.
And feel the power that comes from owning your emotional world.

It feels better to take full responsibility for your choices.
This is what it feels like to be an adult.

And as an adult, you get to decide all of it without having to make any excuses at all.

What are you pretending you don't know?

I had a mystery in my life for years.

I talked about it a lot— over lunch with friends, phone conversations with my sister, emails with my coaching forum.

I was dramatic about the not knowing.
I would exclaim, with great emphasis, "I have absolutely NO IDEA why this is so."
And everyone would agree with me.
It sounded legitimate.

We would go round and round on the mystery.
It looked as if we were addressing the problem.
We were paying so much attention to it.
Dedicating so much time to it.

I never realized that the belief, "I don't know why..."
was blocking me from finding out.

I was never going to know as long as I told myself that I didn't.
That's because we always take actions to prove our beliefs.
This way, we can keep telling ourselves how right we are.

As long as I believed I didn't know the answer, I certainly wouldn't go looking for it.
And so, I didn't.

I just kept spinning in "I-Don't-Know-Land."
It was quite comforting there actually.
It was all childish and victim-y.

I was just waiting there for someone else to figure it out and tell me the answer.

And tell me what to do about it as well.
Or maybe they'd just fix it for me while they were there.

Guess what?
If I had just changed my belief to "I'm going to find out why this is so," I would have skipped some of those lunches and done some detective work.

I didn't need to know exactly what to do or how to find out in order to believe it. All I needed was the belief that I will do what it takes to figure this out.

And guess what?

The answer was as simple as '1+1 does not = 2'.

And that's all I needed to see.

Then the rest of the path to "I do know" became clear.
That's all it took.

"I don't know" is poison.
What are you pretending you don't know?

Because I know.
That you know.
That you are guided.
Just like me. Whenever I believe I am.

You are guided.

We can't always access our own wisdom

I coached a friend who thought she was going through a major catastrophe.

She's also a coach—a brilliant coach, who recently coached me through my own catastrophe.

Here's what's funny...

I simply repeated what she had told me months ago.

She listened intently and wrote everything down.

Then she asked me to send it to her in an email because she didn't get it all.

Do you know what I labelled the email?

"Regurgitation".

I was simply regurgitating her own material.

It's hard to get perspective on our own story because we think it's real. I thought my circumstances were making me feel terrible.

It was clear to her that the way I was choosing to interpret them was causing my devastation.

That my projecting into a catastrophic future was causing my panic. Because she's a brilliant coach, she never once dropped into my story and agreed that what had happened to me was terrible.

But she can't see it for herself.

She knows, because she's a brilliant coach, that it must be her beliefs, but she can't figure out how to get herself out of the strong emotions she's swept herself into.

It feels too real, too oppressive.

For me, because I'm not in it, it's obvious.

She has to remind herself that all she has is this moment.

That nothing bad is happening in this moment.

That the Universe is always conspiring for her (and she doesn't have to know why or how).

Step outside your story.

I coached a friend who thought she was going through a major catastrophe.

She's also a coach—a brilliant coach, who recently coached me through my own catastrophe.

Here's what's funny...

I simply repeated what she had told me months ago.

She listened intently and wrote everything down.

Then she asked me to send it to her in an email because she didn't get it all.

Do you know what I labelled the email?

"Regurgitation".

I was simply regurgitating her own material.

It's hard to get perspective on our own story because we think it's rea I thought my circumstances were making me feel terrible.

It was clear to her that the way I was choosing to interpret them was causing my devastation.

That my projecting into a catastrophic future was causing my panic. Because she's a brilliant coach, she never once dropped into my story and agreed that what had happened to me was terrible.

But she can't see it for herself.

She knows, because she's a brilliant coach, that it must be her beliefs, but she can't figure out how to get herself out of the strong emotions she's swept herself into.

It feels too real, too oppressive.

For me, because I'm not in it, it's obvious.

She has to remind herself that all she has is this moment.

That nothing bad is happening in this moment.

That the Universe is always conspiring for her (and she doesn't have t know why or how).

That every catastrophe can hand us exactly what we need to awaken into who we truly are.

That she can choose.

That she has a choice here.

She's a brilliant coach for me, but for her, she's useless.

As coaches, we are pretty good at self coaching and I always teach my clients how to coach themselves.

But when you're caught off guard and can't find your own deep wisdom, there's no substitute for an outside perspective.

Someone who can see clearly that it is always our own interpretation of what's happening that is causing us to feel horrible.

How will you know? When you can't step outside your own story.

AWAKEN

Who or what is your teacher right now?

"What's happening that you wish wasn't happening?"

That's your teacher.

What is it there to teach you?

The idea that the person/experience in front of me is my teacher is comforting to me. I recently developed Raynaud's Syndrome, which means that fingers and toes freeze when it's cold. It's painful.

I've had to eliminate my outdoor fall and winter walks, and getting food out the freezer requires slippery woollen gloves.
I'm told there's no cure, and I won't take meds.
The best my doctor could do was tell me to move back to South Africa, where it's always warm.

What if this is my teacher right now?

Here's the lesson, and how I learned it -
I told my massage therapist that my feet were frozen.
Usually, when they're frozen, I focus on them a lot because it hurts.
Instead, she asked me if any part of my body was warm.
"Yes. My arms."
"Focus on your arms."

Almost immediately, my feet started to tingle and the iciness started to thaw.

I've tried this many times since. They always start to tingle. Sometimes they thaw completely. Other times they're still numb but it doesn't hurt as much.

Here's what my Raynaud's has taught me so far:
When we focus on what we don't want, whether it's frozen feet, excess weight, or an unlovable boss, we get more of it.

When I focused on my pain, the discomfort remained until I was near a heater.

When we focus on what we do want and find evidence for it some-where in our body or our life, what we want becomes our experience. Even if that unwanted thing doesn't go away, it's no longer what we're focusing on and therefore no longer causing us pain.

Where can you shift your focus from what you don't want to what you do want and already have?

FOUR BE THE TRUE YOU

Does this feel like love?

Whenever I'm faced with a dilemma, I ask myself this question - what would feel like love?

My husband and I were in New Orleans and I was enjoying my seven-kilometer run through the vibrant French Quarter soaking up the sights and sounds when I slipped and fell. I scraped my knees and calf quite badly. Immediately, I wondered if I should stop running.

I'm worthy of my love.

It would be a valid excuse, as I was quite banged up.
I did a quick mental check—

Bones? Intact.

Joints? Still moving.

It was just skin damage.

I checked my feelings in my body—give up?
Not one cell agreed to do it.
I couldn't wait to get started again.
Because running felt like love to me that day.

If I had been running because I wanted to change my body, or punish myself for drinking too much the night before, that would have felt like self-hatred, and I would have jumped at the chance to use the fall as an excuse to stop.

But exercise feels enormously like love to me.

And that's why I do it.

And that's why I choose it over lunch dates, manicures, or sleeping in.

And each time I run, I prove to myself that I'm worthy of my love.

And all other love can only come from that place.

Creating Time and Other Brain Renovations

Did you know you are a time creator? I was sceptical about this idea at first, until I reflected on it. Here's how it works: there are 24 hours in every day, 168 hours in every week, 8,760 hours in every year. Our ability to create time rests in the fact that we decide how we want to spend those hours, each and every one. Therefore, we are creating that time for ourselves.

What would change in your day if you recognized that you were creating every minute of it? Think about what you'd do that you aren't doing. Think about what you're doing now that you would stop doing if you knew that this minute was created by you, for you.

Whenever you think, "I don't have time," you will create a paucity of time. Practice reframing the thought to, "I create as much time as I need," and you will create as much time as you need, because we always prove ourselves right. Time is about choices. If you wish you had more time, stop wasting your time on wishes and start thinking about what you would do with more time. Then, use your brain to start creating the time to do them because you actually do have the time. You're just wasting time believing you don't, and we always prove ourselves right.

Creating time is actually about creating space—space to do what feeds your soul while taking care of your responsibilities. If you are feeling overwhelmed and overscheduled, like many busy people I know, consider what you can put down. It's not going to be what you think. You don't have to cross a thing off your to-do list. You can do it all, as soon as you start believing you can. Your beliefs about time are slowing you down and making you feel overwhelmed, not your list. Give yourself the gift of time right now by making different choices. What time-sucking MENTAL activities can you delegate, delay, or delete entirely?

Create space to free your soul.

These reflections are about creating time and space by renovating your brain. As you read, consider where in your life it's time to adjust your perspective. How can you use your infinitely brilliant mind to ensure that you take full responsibility for whatever you create today, next week, next month?

You CAN do it all. But only if you think you can.

For the first time ever, I decided to do two webinars on a Monday.

I'm a last-minute person, so I didn't plan them the week before. I knew I'd be able to prepare over the weekend because teaching is easy for me. Because I believe this, I create classes quickly. I'm blessed with inspiration just when I need it. But I forgot that I was going away with my husband for a romantic weekend, and we had agreed to leave our laptops at home and unplug our phones other than for check-ins with the kids.

No problem.

I stayed up late the night before the webinars and created the slide show. But first, we took the kids out for dinner and planned a family celebration for the next Wednesday.

That morning, I set up the technology for my webinar in the same way I do for my regular video conferences and I was ready to go. Or so I thought. My first webinar was a technological disaster.

Luckily I had all of Monday afternoon to figure it out before my second webinar. Which I did, thanks to Coach Google, in between baking delicacies for our celebration with my daughter and her friend.

The second webinar was 95% flawless and well-attended. After the webinar – because, again, I'm a last-minute person – I spent much of the night figuring out how to upload my recording to send out to all of my listeners. I have a skilled support team who could do it for me in a second, but unlike me, they were asleep, and I wanted to get the replay to those who couldn't make the webinar live immediately because I truly believe that the information I shared is life changing.

After, at about 2:00 am, I cleaned the kitchen and packed away all the pastries. I didn't even eat any. OK, maybe one. Delicious.
I noticed myself wanting more - many more - we had made a variety of flavours, but I chose to feel light instead.

The next day was a full day of coaching, parenting, kids' basketball games, debate tournaments, and delivering on a promise to watch gymnastics training.

No problem for me.

Here's why.

I know I can do it all.
Because I chose it all.
All of it.

The busy, crazy, fun, endless activity, and fulfilling of obligations and promises.

None of it burdens me.
I know I don't have to do any of it if I don't want to.

And that makes all the difference.

As soon as I acknowledge my active choice, all resistance drops away. I don't have to go to any of the practices or games. I can cancel my clients if I want to. Yes, they'll be disappointed, and the kids may not have a ride home, but no one and nothing is making me do any of it. Yes, I'm tired, and I'll take a nap someday. But the only reason it's not today is that I chose this exact day.

I could have easily found how it's not fair that I have to do it all, or that I should have more help, or that the kids should be more independent, or that I should work less. All of which could be true for me if I wanted to make it true by believing it (and believe me, I spent many years living that painful version).

But instead, I chose this. All of it. Full frontal living. Because it makes me feel alive, engaged, and expansive.

What are you choosing? And how does it make you feel?

Choose full frontal living.

Where are you on your priority list?

There is no right or wrong way to behave—there's only curiosity and fascination with why we do what we do.

When we're creating results in our lives that we aren't happy with, we must find our thoughts and beliefs that lead to us behaving in ways that create these undesirable results.

Two clients texted me at the last minute to reschedule their coaching sessions. Both involved work "emergencies" that they unthinkingly and reflexively put before their own mental wellbeing.

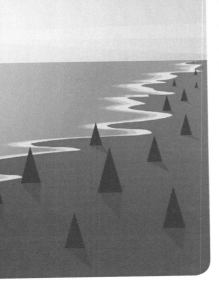

Be curious about why you do what you do.

One, an employee, was asked to attend an urgent meeting during lunch hour, which she unquestioningly agreed to until she texted me. I offered her the option of responding that she had a prior appointment and couldn't make the meeting.

The second, a business owner, received an urgent request from her employee for a phone conversation. She had recently lost her mother and she wanted emotional support. Condolences had already been offered and bereavement leave granted. My client wanted to attend her coaching session, yet she agreed to call her employee, until I offered her the option of prioritizing her own emotional and mental wellbeing.

Both clients always fulfilled their responsibilities in their workplaces, and I was curious about why they failed to fulfill their responsibilities to themselves as women who want to live more evolved, gratifying, and conscious lives.

For me, it's neutral—I don't lose when a client cancels a session. Coaching is all about the client—it is their weekly haven when they enter an unconditionally loving space knowing they can be whoever they are and will never be judged.

Hiring a coach is an act of extreme self-care, and I believe that everyone should do it. So cancelling a coaching session is an act of neglecting yourself—it's like cancelling your self-care.

What's fascinating to me is that both clients were upset that they 'had' to cancel, but neither even considered that they had a choice.

This led to an interesting discussion about priorities, and I want to offer you this exercise:
List your top 5 priorities in order of importance.

Options include: your physical, emotional, spiritual, and mental wellbeing; family; finances; career/business; community; friends; studying; service.

I recommend that you put yourself at the top because your well-being is required in order to be able to meet all the other priorities.

Then go back to last week's schedule and assess whether your calendar aligns with your priorities. Read your emails and texts and evaluate whether your responses reflect your priorities.

This was an eye-opening exercise for both of my clients. Career/business landed as the third priority for one client and fourth for the other.

We became curious about why they had responded to a demand from a lower priority at the expense of their highest priority. Both clients gained insight into the reason they were feeling unfulfilled and stressed at work. They had been taking actions that weren't in line with what's truly important to them. Once they knew, they could decide consciously, what they wanted to create in their lives

It's not easy to tell a mourning employee they will have to wait an hour to get emotional support from you, especially when you've been a people-pleaser all your life.

It's not easy to tell your boss you can't come to the lunchtime appointment, especially when you've also been a people-pleaser all your life.

But evolving into your highest and best self isn't always easy. Nor is ignoring your deepest desire to do so.

Evolve into your highest self.

It's so worth it.

It's far better to honour your desire to meet with your coach, and then, feeling refuelled and authentic, call and offer your heartfelt, resentment-free support to your employee, or to return from your lunchtime coaching session refreshed and energized, catch up on the meeting, and take care of your duties without battling frustration and disappointment.

Everyone wins when you live according to your priorities. You first.

It's the opposite of selfish; it's the most loving and giving thing you can do for your people and your world.

Are you worth the time?

I was surrounded by beauty. A salad in the making. Organic produce supplied by local farmers.

It was the first week of my biannual cleanse—fresh fruits and veggies all day—yum! This meant lots of chopping, slicing, washing, steaming, roasting, souping (yes, us soup addicts believe making soup deserves it's own verb!). It takes time, and I always have exactly enough time to do what I want to do.

This is not the case for most of my clients.
They tell me that they don't have time to "shop for or prepare nourishing foods, or even to sit down and eat their meals. I help them discover that they're lying to themselves. Every time.

How do I know this?
The women who tell me they have no time to do what they want to do range from full-time working mothers with no help in the house to grandmothers who have no dependents and don't work outside the home. The mom believes that if she had no children to look after, she would have tons of time. Tell that to the granny.

I fall somewhere in between—entrepreneur, mother of four children, growing team of household help. I'm always scheduled mom. I only do things I want to do, and I always have enough time to do them.

Before you install a shrine to me, let me tell you that as I prepare my delicious salad, the monthly bills are waiting to be paid, my children's dental appointments are overdue, and my son is wearing the same pants he wore yesterday.

It's not that I don't want to do the laundry, pay the bills, or make appointments. I do and I will. It's just that right now I want to make the salad more. And I'm doing it without inner conflict.

I fully believe that my body deserves delicious food and everything that follows will be done more easily because my mind won't be 'busy' telling me how bad I am for grabbing cookies instead of making a salad.

When my clients and I explore their excuse of having no time, we often uncover their belief that they're not worthy. Not worthy of taking the time to feed themselves well. Not worthy of taking the time to care for themselves. Although I do have many unhelpful beliefs I've conjured up over the years, I do believe I'm worthy (and for this a resounding 'thank you' to my parents).

YOU DESERVE ALL OF IT.

As a coach, one of the gifts I offer is to call out my clients when they tell themselves painful lies.

Because I believe that they're worthy.
Of telling themselves the truth. Of the time, the money, and the effort to do what it takes to feel good, healthy, and vibrant.

And the only way to get to that conversation is to drop the "I don't have enough time" story.
Tell the truth.
It's a cover-up.
It's a lie.
And it doesn't serve you.

Our thoughts create our result. Every time we think, "I don't have enough time," we feel overwhelmed, tired, and hopeless. From this place, we'll be disorganized, waste time, talk to our friends about being too busy, and end up not having enough time.

Not good for us. Not good for our family.
The greatest gift you can give your family is your own happiness. My client discovered that

"I deserve..." thoughts make her happy:

"I deserve to eat nutritious food."

"I deserve to be well hydrated."

"I deserve to take good care of myself."

"I deserve to spend money on myself."

And these thoughts make her feel happy and they remind her to make the time.

What works for you?

When something feels urgent, take it as a sign that you need to slow down

Let's talk about hurrying, or rather, not hurrying in order to arrive speedily and effectively.

When we act speedily with a clear mind, we accomplish our goals effectively and efficiently.

But when we rush with a sense of urgency, we sometimes lose our way, or trip over ourselves, or get to the end and discover it's not where we wanted to be at all.

My client, Clara, has been acting from a sense of urgency for a long time. We explored some recent examples and discovered that when she acts on something quickly and believes it's urgent, it usually doesn't serve her in the long run.

She:
Stuffed as much food into her mouth as quickly as she could before someone could see her.

Chased after someone to tell them how they wronged her.

Ordered three purses during an online flash sale.

All of these actions ended in regret, and she's wondering how to avoid this in future. Easily, I told her. Pay attention to how you're feeling.

Why don't you try this as you read?
Think of a time when you were rushed and believed you needed to do something urgently.
Got it?
Now turn your attention to your body—how does it feel?

How does 'urgent' feel in your body?
For Clara, it felt tight and also fast. This compelled her to act quickly to get rid of the uncomfortable sensation. But in its place, she found remorse and regret, which are just as uncomfortable in a different, slow, and sluggish way.

Has this happened to you, too? Do you do that urgent thing and then immediately wish you hadn't? Replacing one uncomfortable feeling with another is not an effective way to relieve discomfort, is it?

I have a much better solution for you: Slow down.
As fast as you want to go, slow yourself down twice as much.
If you want to stuff six truffles in your mouth at once, eat only one.

If you want to run and chase the offender, make yourself walk slowly. If you're breathing fast, make yourself breathe in for a count of six and out for a count of six. If you're scared you'll lose those online purses, make yourself type with only one finger. One keystroke a second.

Here's why:
I believe that our natural state is calm and peaceful. So any time we are feeling urgent and rushed, it's because we are telling ourselves a lie.
"I have to binge in secret so I won't feel ashamed."
"He has to apologize so I can feel better."
"I have to take advantage of this bargain."

As I typed those sentences for Clara, my heart started to beat faster and my stomach tightened, and they weren't even my thoughts.
Such an uncomfortable way to be. And all lies. The truth is that if all she wants is to feel better, she doesn't need to stuff that food in her mouth, or extract an apology, or snag a bargain. All she has to do is slooooooooow herself down. Relax her clenched body. Slow her heartbeat and buzzing mind.
Then, she will know.

"It doesn't matter if they see what I ate. I'm the only one who can make me feel ashamed."

"A forced apology won't mean anything. I can make myself feel better right now."

"There's always another bargain. Debt never feels good."

Now imagine taking all these actions from a sense of calm and peace. You pick the perfect looking truffle and place it on a plate. Just as you're about to eat it, your family comes home. You know it's yours and you can eat it whenever you want to. You know your worth has nothing to do with what you eat. You save it for later when the house is quiet and you can enjoy it.

Mmmmm.

How about you? Retrace that action you took in such a hurry. What if you had decided to slow it down? Wait until tomorrow? Would it have mattered? What were you thinking that made you feel urgent? Now, in hindsight, did that thinking serve you? Did your need to be right, or first, give you the feeling you wanted?

I love the idea of moving quickly AND not rushing. It feels like the difference between frantic speed walking and long deep strides.
We'll cover the same distance in the same time, but we get to choose whether we'll get there calm and relaxed, or tight and clenched. And we're much less likely to have done damage along the way, and much more likely to have noticed the flowers in our path.

What do you make your age mean?

I am fabulously fifty years old!
I don't usually pay much attention to numbers, but turning fifty felt important. Like it needed to be marked. I felt the energy building for something powerful.

On my 50th birthday, it revealed itself.

Fifty will be the decade I let go of other people's opinions.
I believe they will become invisible to me. Unnoticeable. Not real at all. This is easily done, once I decide to do it, because other people's opinions only exist in their minds, which makes them completely unreal to my mind, unless I decide to seek them out and pay attention to them.

My youngest daughter said "Mommy, I feel like since you were 45 you've gone backwards, so now you're more like 40."
And she's right. I feel it too.
At 45, I learned the tools to effortlessly and joyfully shed almost 60 pounds. More importantly, I have shed ten times that in emotional baggage.

After a decade of looking for peace in other people, like energy healers, yogis, and fellow seekers, I discovered that what I was seeking resided within me. It had always been there, but I had to go through many rings of fire to find it. And I learned how to do the hard work of staying with myself during excruciating emotional pain and intense joy (which is often equally challenging) to get there.

It's no wonder I look and feel younger at 50 than I did at 40.

And now I sense a whole other transformation coming. I'm moving beyond my conditioning to my authentic self. She operates based on her values and inner guidance. And allows others to operate, undisturbed and unjudged, by their own compasses. She understands that her freedom, her peace, and what is best for her, will ultimately be best for all concerned.

It's already begun – it began on my 50th birthday. I was at lunch with my husband, parents, and sister, when a singer arrived to serenade me with lyrics written just for me to the tune of the song from our first dance at our wedding.

It was a small, quiet cafe—only two other parties, until the singer arrived, and stayed, and sang, and sang, channeling Frank Sinatra and Elvis to entice my mom and my sister to join in. After, my mom said it was lucky that the other parties didn't mind. I was quite surprised when she mentioned this. I hadn't even noticed that anyone else was there. During the thoughtful and touching performance, just for me, I opened to the whole experience—the love shining from my husband as I enjoyed it, the twinkle in my mom's eyes as she joined in.
We were all that existed.

This is how my fifties will be. I will live in the love. The beauty. The joy. The intensity of the moment. I will act and react from my deepest truth.

I shine with anticipation of what further truths I will discover as I delve closer and closer to my authentic self with all the gifts she has to share.

I WILL ACT AND REACT
FROM MY DEEPEST TRUTH

At what age are your personality, habits, and behaviour permanently fixed?

At whatever age you choose.

How do I know this?

Because you will create that reality for yourself in two ways:

CREATE YOUR REALITY

1. When you reach this age, your belief that you are now carved in stone will result in you thinking and behaving in your habitual way, even if your circumstances and opportunities change.

2. You will continually scan your environment for evidence that this is true, and you will find it.

My friend Denise was never athletic or active. She would have laughed at me if I had suggested we go for a run together. Then at the age of 44, Denise hired a personal trainer.

This trainer believed that Denise could run and put her on the treadmill, set it for a running speed, and told her to run for five minutes.
Because Denise did not believe that she was too old to change, she started running. The trainer gradually increased her time, and she's now running continuously for 14 minutes. She is immensely proud of herself.

If she had believed that she was too old to become a runner, too old to change, too old to try something new, as many people in their forties do believe, she would never have had the wonderful experience of going running with her 11-year-old daughter three months later.

She was willing to change her belief that "I'll never be a runner" because she did not hold the belief that "I'm too old for this."

Have you reached the age at which you believe you have lost your chance? Carved in stone? Too old to change?

Do you want to live the rest of your life based on this belief?

If not, simply add at least 20 years to the age you have chosen to believe marks you as 'set' (yes, this includes no matter how old you are), then look for evidence that this new number could be true.
Use Denise as your evidence.

NOW...
Go out and create your own evidence.

Five steps to a brain renovation

I did a brain renovation and literally turned my entire thinking around in order to get what I wanted.

Did you know that you create all your results in your life with your brain?

What I mean is, we are always creating evidence for what we believe, so when we want something, we first have to believe we can get it and then we go about creating it. Sometimes it seems as if it just happened to us, or someone else gave it to us, but if you trace it back, you will find that you first conceived of it with your brain—by thinking about it and wanting it and believing it was possible.

I received a business offer that went beyond my dreams. If I accepted, it would take my business to the next level, and enable me to exceed my financial goals for the year. My first response was to reject it. Well, half of it. I said I could maybe do half.

When I ended the meeting, I believed that I had to decline the offer because it would require more time than I devote to my business right now and all my other time is spoken for. I'm helping my son heal from Crohn's Disease through a diet which requires all his food to be made from scratch, and I am an involved mother of four kids who eat a lot and make a lot of messes! I also work out, bond regularly with family and friends, and dedicate time to learning and study each week. In short, I lead a full and wonderful life with few blank spaces on my calendar. But at the same time, I had a business goal to meet, and it was a big one.

My brain, in its current state, was not able to see how to do all of this, so it caused me to say no to the offer that would enable me to realize my business dream. Makes no sense, right?

A brain renovation.

I see the same thing with my weight loss clients. They create an eating plan that has them losing weight and feeling energetic and then their brain, in its current state, starts to object and protest. They question the validity of the science I present, worry about their protocol, and refuse to believe it could be a permanent solution, even though they desperately want it to be.

All that's needed is a brain renovation.

Our beliefs are strong connections in our brain, and the problem is we think they are facts and truths, so we keep operating within them. I believed I couldn't devote more hours to my business than I already do and I thought it was true until I woke up the next morning and realized that although all my son's food has to be made in my kitchen, it doesn't have to be me who makes it.

And that was the small brain renovation that led to a different outcome for me.

My twice-a-week housekeeper walked into the house, I offered her another two days of work each week, she beamed, we hugged, I accepted the business offer, and I am well on my way to exceeding my business goal.

You can renovate your brain too, and it can be way less painful than a home renovation.

All it takes is a willingness to be wrong:

1. Think about something you want and list all the reasons you can't have it.

2. Look at your list with a sceptical eye.

3. Notice how all your reasons are simply thoughts and beliefs.

4. Find where and how you are wrong.

5. Demolish and update the wrong bits.

And you'll instantly see your way to achieving your dream.

I'm not disorganized anymore!

I'd been telling myself I'm disorganized for much of my life.

My hyper-organized oldest daughter agreed and reinforced this belief every time I forgot to pick a child up from school (yep – it happened a few times) or couldn't find something she needed immediately.

I described it as a character flaw.

I'd thought this so many times that I had begun to believe it was real. Fixed. Something in me that I would have to manage and compensate for with all my other sparkling traits. Of course, this isn't true.

When I would tell friends that I was disorganized, some would be shocked and tell me all the ways they thought I was a disciplined person. Hard to create a successful business all on your own and run a busy household of six (with only the occasional forgotten child) without any organizational skills, right?

When I held a magical retreat in Imperial Beach, California, we started the event by choosing something we wanted to release from our lives. I chose to release my belief that I was a disorganized person. All our results in our lives derive from our thoughts and beliefs because the way we think influences the way we feel, and the way we feel determines what we'll do, which of course creates our results.

So, being in a heightened state of awareness, thanks to the magical surroundings and the glorious company at the retreat,

I remembered that it was just a belief I'd created in my mind, and decided to be done with it.

I knew that the more I told myself I was disorganized, the more papers, items, and children I would lose. I threw it into the sea, yelled it at the top of my lungs, and kind of forgot about it.

A few months after my retreat, as I drove home on time with all four kids accounted for, and entered my neat and tidy house, with all (OK, most) papers filed, I realized that I'm no longer a disorganized person. Sure, sometimes I forget stuff, but rarely. And sometimes I choose Netflix over a clean kitchen, which means I go to bed later than planned, but then I clean it in the morning, and mostly, these days, I'm pretty functionally organized.

RELEASE

How much emotional baggage do you carry around in your bag?

Along my journey to end my weight loss struggle, I often found myself overburdened with options I had packed "just in case." Do you find that? Are you stressed about "what if" questions—like "What if I'm hungry and there is nothing healthy to eat?" Or perhaps it is in other areas of your life like, "What if my luggage gets lost?"

One time, I took an overnight trip to a wedding with my daughter. I knew there would be a lavish wedding meal, followed by brunch the next day, and then home. But in addition to all our clothes, makeup, and accessories, I arrived with a full bag of food: dried fruit, protein bars, fresh fruit, fresh veggies, herbal tea bags—for our 16-hour stay. On arrival, we were also presented with a huge gift basket full of delicious things to eat in our hotel room. Needless to say, I repacked all this food to take it home the next day!

I felt foolish. I felt overloaded.

I do this with personal activities too—my carry-on bag is bigger than my children's. Every trip, I take knitting, needlepoint, laptop, iPad, books, and a stack of magazines.

I tell myself I don't have to do it all; I just like to know they're there if I want to. Just in case.

It's a lie I'm telling myself. All that food. All that stuff. It makes me feel weighed down.

Does this sound like you? What's in your bag? How do you feel about the contents of your bag when you unpack it?

Sometimes it takes a while to find the answer. I struggled with that question. Having mastered the art of backpacking across two continents in my twenties, I take great pleasure in packing the minimum clothing needed. Why do I burden myself with food every time I travel?

I discussed this with my coach, and she asked me a question that changed my life. "Which do you prefer—travelling light or having choices?" By working with my coach, I was able to understand that I could find the freedom I needed to make the right choices—not by relying on having something with me to deal with every possible scenario, but by being able to make the right choice based on the options around me at the time and leaving lots of room for thoughts of abundance, not restrictions.

These days, I board planes carrying only a purse.

Contents:

1 novel

1 laptop

1 protein bar

1 wallet

1 phone

That's it.
No emotional baggage.
I love it.

Answer: Travelling light.   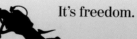   It's freedom.

What are you dressed for today?

My husband and I were driving home from an appointment and I was wondering aloud whether I'd be able to fit in my workout today, even though it was a day I don't work in my business. "Why not?" he asked.

I listed everything I needed to accomplish in the hour and a half before I took my daughter to her appointment. After that, teaching, coaching, more pickups, more drop-offs, prepare dinner for the kids, and gussy up for a fancy event downtown with said hubby. He looked at me sympathetically (and admiringly, I like to think, for how much I do in a day):

"Maybe the workout won't happen today, huh?"

But then I looked out the car. It was a perfect spring day with a clear blue sky, slight breeze, sun shining, birds singing.

"I don't want to miss this beautiful day," I said
We were just passing near our house.
"Why don't I drop you here and you can jog home through the ravine?" he asked.

"I love you," I said. "You're a genius!"
As I hopped out of the car and started my jog through the gorgeous ravine, I thought, "I'm a genius!" as I noticed that I was wearing my workout clothes. Even though I didn't have a workout scheduled for that day, my higher self had intended, all along, that I was going to enjoy the gorgeous day and get some exercise.

Because the intention was set, the HOW made itself apparent to me. All I had to do was grab the moment. It means everything else will be a bit rushed. It means I'll do my makeup on the subway tonight (remember that childhood trick—if you look down and don't see them, they won't see you? It works on full subway cars too). If I'd had to go home and change, those extra few minutes would have made my workout a nonstarter.

When you're getting dressed, be conscious about the intention you're setting for the day you want to create. If baggy sweats and oversized T-shirts are your daily garb, ask yourself if this is in alignment with your intention for your days, which become your life.

That night, I intended to dazzle my husband and his associates at our fancy event.
How did I dress?
I started with my slinky new python-skin stilettos, that's for sure.

How do you get what you want?

There are lots of ways to get what you want.
One way is to give it to yourself.
Then you get exactly what you want.
No mistakes.

I tried another way this Mother's Day. I asked.
Specifically.
I even sent him the link to the exact supplier I love.

And guess what?
Mother's Day morning, breakfast in bed.
Squeals of delight.
The exact beeswax candle I wanted.
Happiness all round.

I used to wait to see if he knew. Maybe I'd drop some hints. Maybe I'd purposefully say nothing to see if he was telepathic, if he remembered. Various ways of testing that didn't serve me or him. Didn't feel good.

I realized that I was putting a high value on him reading my mind. Like lovers do in movies, and fairy tales, and romance novels. But when I thought about it, what I want from my lover is that he listens to me. Hears me. Derives pleasure from getting me exactly what I want.

Well, if that's what's important to me from my husband, I need to tell him so he has the possibility of fulfilling this desire I have of him. The outcome was so much better than playing subversive testing games.

It was clean.

I said what I wanted.

He knew what I wanted.

I got what I wanted.

That's another way of getting what you want. With a big slice of loving and "feel good" all around.

SAY WHAT YOU WANT

Are you holding yourself back with your mind?

In Canada we celebrate Family Day on the third Monday in February. It's a great opportunity to sleep in, stay warm inside with my crazy gang, and skip school lunches.

The next day I mistakenly arrived for what I thought was my regular Monday 10:00am yoga class. But it wasn't my usual crowd in the studio.

My classmates were young and muscular. My neighbour confirmed my fear—it was a Power Flow class (Tuesday schedule. Of course).

It's not that I haven't done Power Flow classes—I used to do them all the time. But since I lost my beloved mother, I'd been gentle with myself. My movement was slower—mostly distance walking. That February I decided to resume my daily workouts, but I told myself that I couldn't do strenuous exercise yet.

And I believed myself.

I had been yearning for hot yoga, so I limited myself to the entry-level classes, even though I was becoming quite bored. Sitting in my Power Flow class on Tuesday, I had a momentary panic, as these classes are intense and demanding. But I decided to stay and follow the teacher's reassurance that "as long as you're breathing, you're practicing yoga."

I reminded myself of a thought I used when I was just starting to exercise:

"I can do anything for one hour," although I didn't believe it this time, and this was a 75-minute class!

All that drama in my head. Unnecessary.

I flowed, I planked, balanced, head stood, sweated, and was surprised when it was already time for final relaxation. And I rediscovered the exhilaration that follows a workout where you push yourself beyond what your mind says you can do.

Pure joy.

I've been depriving myself of that exhilaration, simply because I believed my own lie. The only thing holding me back from this joy was my mind.

What will I gain from this?

One of my clients was deciding what food she would give up permanently after our annual cleanse. After a previous cleanse, she'd eliminated caffeine and diet soda, and wanted to extend her success.

I suggested she reframe her question. Every time I cleanse, I ask myself, *"What will I gain this time?"*

I'm happy to report that in my last cleanse, I reconnected with my creativity. For years I'd been advised by various healers and coaches to reconnect with my creativity. Writing this book feels creative and soul-filling for me. I also took an art journaling class with some friends and the glee I felt when I picked up my first paint brush since school hinted at the joy that creativity would bring to my life.

In this last cleanse, I found it in cooking.

I'd always been a cleanse nerd. And a recipe nerd. I followed directions to the fine print if I chose to do it. I'd been known to drive to five stores for the ingredients for one recipe. And I've always marveled at my sister-in-law who conjures delicious dishes from what's in the kitchen. I need marvel no more. I'm one of them now. For the first time in my life, I created fantastic dishes based on the huge pile of fresh veggies overflowing from my fridge and shared them with my class.

So much fun.
Creativity.
Soul-filling.
Nourishing.
Community-creating.

I believe that if I'd gone into the cleanse thinking about everything I had to give up—processed food, sugar, caffeine, dairy, wheat - I wouldn't have found this. I may have made up some new recipes, sure. But I wouldn't have connected this action with my intention to find what's new here for me. And I wouldn't have related it to my soul's quest to connect with my creativity.

CONNECT WITH CREATIVITY

I learn something new every cleanse, which always feels connected to the nourishment of my body, my mind, and my soul.

What if we approached everything we've chosen to do with this question: What will I gain from this? Especially things we think we won't enjoy. What will you gain from this?

Maybe it's the holidays with the entire warring family in one house.
What will I gain from this?

Maybe it's spending the holidays alone.
What will I gain from this?

A separation, a hard class, a tough project, a new baby, marriage...
What will I gain from this?

And also everything we haven't explicitly chosen.

Being fired.
What will I gain from this?

Someone leaving, someone dying, getting sick.
What will I gain from this?

What do you wish you never did anymore?

I used to text while driving.
Yes, I admit it. Not proud of it.

Actually, I still do it sometimes. I'm a bit addicted. I said I'm not proud. So, I tried a new technique. I started telling it like I want it to be instead of how it is. Every time I noticed myself checking a text or typing one, I'd put the phone down and say, "I used to text while driving."

It was an interesting experiment. Every time I did it, I felt a slight shift inside me. As if it was becoming true.

You may be surprised—my clients and students know that I'm a bit obsessive about telling it like it is. I don't let many untruths get by me when I'm coaching or teaching. I believe that the truth sets us free and always feels better. But this felt right somehow.

I told myself what I wanted to be my truth. The difference is I knew I would still do it. I wasn't lying to myself or pretending I was clean of this habit. I was aware that I was telling it how I wanted it to be.

And I think it worked. While I still pick up my phone, I put it down almost immediately.

And I think that the next step is to find the pause between thinking about sending a text and picking up the phone. During that pause, I'll remember that I used to text while driving and don't anymore. And I won't even pick it up.

Some of my students tried it with social media. The minute they realized they were in the middle of a mindless scroll, they told themselves, "I used to do social media instead of living my real life." Some found that it helped them stop scrolling in a peaceful and natural way, which is always the goal for me.

Struggling does not change behaviour.

I don't believe that struggling is an effective way to change behaviour.

Try it.

Practice believing that you used to do that thing you wish you no longer did. You will probably make it your reality.

Positive thinking can get you positive results

My favourite part of being a coach is where I don't believe what my clients tell me.

They think something is a fact. True. Immovable. And so they think that the best they can do is find a way to feel better about this fact. And sometimes that is the case—for example, a cancer diagnosis or a death.

But most of the time, what they think is a concrete truth is just a belief, and the only thing keeping them stuck in this situation is their belief that it's true.

I hope that makes sense to you—it's quite a mouthful.

You've probably heard about the power of positive thinking. The idea that all you need is positive thinking to get you what you want may be annoying to you. Please stay with me because what I'm talking about is different than the idea that all you need to do is think it, feel it, and it will magically appear from a mysterious, divine source.I'm not knocking this idea. It's just that that's not what I'm talking about.

What I want to offer you is that if you choose positive thinking, that you believe, you will be more likely to create exactly what you want.

Let me demonstrate with a recent client example: Noreen's daughter was about to start university. She was all set to go—accepted by her college of choice and deposits paid. This amazing girl would thrive in the right environment and with the right supports. But Noreen recently discovered that this college (College A) wouldn't be the best fit for her daughter. She found College B, which seemed ideal. Too late (she believed).

She asked me to help her find a way to think about this that would reduce her anxiety and guilt. She wanted to use positive thinking to feel better about what she thought was a done deal.

I asked Noreen why she's sending her daughter to a college that she believes is unsuitable. Especially given the fact that College B was willing to accept her daughter.

She had convincing reasons.
"My daughter picked College A."
"My husband liked it best."
"College B may not have freshman housing for her."
And on and on.

When I asked her how these reasons felt to her, they all felt some version of negative. But she still didn't believe that it was possible to change. Too many hurdles. It's a done deal.

Negative thinking is always going to get you negative results.

Here's why: when you believe that something is a done deal, even if you hate that idea, you will find evidence for its immutability everywhere.

Noreen raised the topic tentatively with her daughter, she didn't even mention it to her husband, she talked to College B, but reported back only on the problems, and she picked unsupportive friends to discuss it with.
And the end result was that she couldn't see an opening to make a change.

Negative thinking will get you negative results, not because some higher power will swoop down and punish you for your lack of faith, but because you will be looking at the situation from that place of negativity and will find all the reasons for your current negative belief.

All I needed to do was not believe Noreen.

I didn't try to convince her that there was a positive option here. All I needed to do was keep questioning her thinking and show her that what she believed was True, Settled, Fact, was simply her opinion.

When someone doesn't believe something we tell them, we have two choices: we can stand firm in our beliefs and try to convince them about it, or we can open up to the possibility that if Bev doesn't see it my way, maybe, just maybe, it's not fact and maybe there's another way here.

Noreen chose the second option. It took a few weeks, but she kept opening herself to positive thinking about this situation.

Negative thinking gets you negative results.

She kept sending me stalled updates, and I persisted in my conviction that this was not evidence that it was a done deal.

Eventually, she saw an opening. A possibility for positive thinking about this. And that changed everything. She saw how she needed to negotiate with her daughter. She saw what she needed to tell her husband. She kept talking to the admissions officer.

Last week, she flew her daughter to College B and deposited her in her freshman dorm. She told me, "It was because you didn't believe me. That's all it took to open my mind to possibility. The 'how' kind of took care of itself then. It was hard and intense, but once my thinking changed, the outcome kind of became inevitable."

What do you need to find positive thinking for in your life?

Maybe you don't believe you can create a six-figure business and have time to rest and relax? I promise you that if you believe this, you will make it true. Negative thinking will create negative results, remember?

Luckily the opposite is equally true:

Positive thinking will create positive results.

Try this:

"Maybe I can love my business and myself enough to create time for both."

or

"Maybe it's possible that rest and relaxation are key to building my six-figure business."

If this feels like an opening for you, try it.

You never know what possibilities will become clear to you. You may schedule a meditation class before your work day. Or you may be efficient during your work day because you have fun dinner plans. Either way, you're more likely to create your six-figure business from ease, simply because you decided to believe it was possible.

Words have the power to create your reality—use them with care

Do you know what words you're allowing to create your reality?

The words that you allow to dominate your consciousness tend to materialize. So, it's a good idea to pay attention to what you're telling yourself all day.

I like to purposefully choose the words I focus on, so I choose sentences that describe the reality I want to create, and then I think them all day. This is the art of believing on purpose

It's how we create new pathways in our brains, so that we change our behaviour without having to fight against our old programming. For example, Gina was about to watch the third hour of Netflix, but when she remembered her sentence, "I'm the kind of person who looks after herself," she lost interest and walked away. Her words became her reality.

Lately, I've been experimenting with single words.
What if you could find one word that, when you think it, would immediately turn your focus to where you want to be?
Wouldn't that be great?
Just one word to keep bringing you back, back, back.
Back to your centred place.
And what would that word be?

For me, it's REMEMBER.

Remember

I've had many insights and epiphanies in my life. I usually live by them for a few weeks or days, and I feel amazing and alive and purposeful, and I get stuff done. And then I forget, and go back to my unconscious life. Lately, every time I notice myself drifting, I simply say "REMEMBER" and all the wisdom and desire helps me turn toward who I want to be.

This inspired me to host an art workshop for my local clients, where we created stunning canvasses with our words. Trust. Care. Lean. Remember.

Lean. Isn't that interesting? You might think that would be a negative word for an emotional eater.

But here's how my student explained it

"I want a lean life. Lean body, lean house (free of clutter and excess), lean friends (only those who fill me)."

Lean

I adore it. I've been thinking about this word ever since.
Lean.
Constraint.
Only what's necessary, helpful, and life-enhancing.
I love it.
What would your word be? That one word that, when you say it,
will bring you right back to your centre?

Give yourself some time to let it come.
You'll know it because the minute you think it, your body will shift—
you'll feel an opening, clarity, maybe even a small tingle.
That's it—that's your word.

JUST ONE WORD

Hold it close and find the magic in it.

Feeling gratitude is an act of self-care. When we slow down long enough to appreciate the things we have—from reading glasses to technology that helps us live better lives, from family who love us to thoughts that can bring us warmth on the coldest of days—we ground ourselves in the present moment.

Consider all the grief we cause ourselves. We create shame, envy, fear, anger, and more. We have control of how we feel in any given moment, and when we choose to be grateful instead of dwelling on the negative, we quickly train ourselves to find the breathtaking moments even on a regular Wednesday afternoon.

I don't always remember to practice gratitude. But whenever I move away from that feeling, something calls me back, and I use the wisdom of my mind to find it. It's one of the most powerful thought exercises we can use. And the best part about it is that it's available to us every moment.

Remember, your past is not a prison.

What are you grateful for in the present?

What are you grateful for in the present?

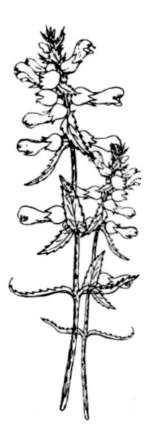

What do you choose to love and appreciate today?

I've developed a kind of embarrassing habit - I kiss things I love.

It all started when I heard this from Abraham: *"Feel your way, little by little, into a greater sense of abundance by noticing things you already have that please you."*

I loved this when I first read it, and started revelling in my memory foam mattress, my green iPhone, my childrens' cheeks (super squishy and yummy), and other things I have and love, but hadn't focused on being grateful for before.

I was shopping with my nephew, and he unexpectedly bought me a stunning bottle of honey that I'd been admiring—unrefined, golden, in a trendy artisan glass bottle.

I kissed the bottle in the store. A little embarrassing, I know.

Now I know what you're thinking. "There's nothing about kissing inanimate objects in this teaching". I know. But I can't explain it.

Next thing I knew, I was getting such great pleasure from the small things I own that I started to kiss them.
Alone.
In my house.

Not in stores.
Yes.
I know.
I'll try not to do that again.

Until recently, I was one of the few people my age who didn't need glasses for reading. I kind of liked that, especially when my younger sister got a pair! But lately, the screen had become slightly blurry, my needlepoint canvas was feeling daunting, and when my daughter asked me to undo the knot in her necklace chain (my specialty), I couldn't see clearly enough to do it.
Bingo!

I remembered the glasses I'd bought during my last pregnancy, when my eyesight deteriorated temporarily.

Sometimes my memory wows me. And that night, not only did I remember I had the glasses, I actually knew where they were.

I kissed my reading glasses, unfolded them, put them on, and wowza!! The knot was crystal clear as was my computer monitor, and I was enormously grateful for this tiny miracle of glass and metal.

What I'm even more grateful for is that I have no resistance to the need for glasses, nor the fact that they signal that my body is aging. Like my mattress and my daughter's soft squishy cheeks, I'm immensely grateful for this body I was given. The body that is working exactly as it's supposed to be working, and looks exactly as it's supposed to look (glass/metal prosthesis and all). The body that houses my soul and my mind, and enables me to do whatever I'm supposed to be doing.

So what if last year I could see perfectly with no assistance? So what if last year there were no tiny lines signaling wrinkles on the way? So what if last decade my upper arms didn't move when I did? That was all exactly as it was supposed to be then. And now this is exactly as it is supposed to be.

And with this belief, the only possible emotion is gratitude, which results in abundance leading to more gratitude and more abundance. And with this cycle firmly in place, I'll be the crazy lady kissing in animate objects all over the world for a long time to come!

What is taking your breath away? Right now?

My brother decided to take our extended family on a sumptuous vacation where an army of people lined up daily to serve our needs and whims. All we had to do was show up and enjoy ourselves.

My brother told me that he was inspired to take us by an idea his friend shared: "It's not how many breaths you take. It's how many moments take your breath away."

We had many breathtaking moments in the first 24 hours we were there. Mostly to do with interactions and lovings. Twelve cousins reunited, sang songs together, danced, rolled down the snow-covered hill, invented games, took care of each other, and blended into each other so you couldn't tell who belonged to who.

Thing is, we could have easily missed all those moments if we were complaining that our rooms had the wrong view, noticing that someone didn't greet us with enough fervour, or arguing about our different philosophies.

Which brings me to my inspiration for you. I turned to my brother and said,

"Those 'take your breath away' moments are always available to us. In every moment. All we need to do is open our eyes to see them."

Now that was probably not the most self-serving thing to tell him. I should have been encouraging him to invite my family to help create breathtaking moments in as many luxurious locales as he can think of!

But it's what I want to tell you.

Right now. Look up. Find the thing that's right in front of you.

Specifically designed to take your breath away.

Right now. For you.

To find.

RIGHT NOW. FOR YOU

I love tricks that make me even better

When I'm in total acceptance of myself and whatever I do, I talk about my mistakes and failures, which often results in me learning strategies for avoiding them in the future.

I interrupted a phone conversation with my brother to take a call from the Expedia representative I'd been holding for.

'I had booked two different tickets to Dallas for a coaching event, and had forgotten to cancel one of them within the 24-hour refund period.' I begged the Expedia representative for leniency, which I didn't receive, so I was left with a $1062 credit with Air Canada, plus a $100 exchange fee when I use it.

I told my brother about it when I called him back and I'm thrilled that I did because he gave me a gift, which, lucky you, I'm going to share— He sets an alarm for 23 hours in advance of the cancellation deadline and labels it "cancel tickets."

LABELS it??

Did you even KNOW you could label your alarms??

Man, I love technology.

My memory is unreliable. I honestly forget about what I've promised to do almost the minute I say, "I will." I make lists, I set reminders, I put it on my calendar.

Effectiveness—about 60%. Because sometimes I just ignore my calendar or reminders.

Come on, I know you do too.

Now I don't even have to try to remember to check my calendar and it's impossible to ignore my alarm.

Here's what I've been doing:
I set alarms with my favourite songs (Yep. You can choose songs for your alarms, too). and every now and then, a song starts to play, which makes me happy, and as I go to turn off the alarm, it tells me what to do.

12:54 pm Cancel Airbnb

2:00 pm Return suits

7:00 pm Bring $5 for Eden to pay Ani

9:00 pm Get Eden from camp reunion

How wonderful is this life? Now, you may think I'm just writing to teach you this memory hack and I do want to share it with you.

But there's another reason I'm telling you about this—Shame.

Many people I know would have been too ashamed to talk about this because they'd think they should have remembered to call and cancel.

They would make it mean something shameful about themselves.

As a life coach, I know that's not true. I choose to believe that it was meant to happen exactly how it happened because it did. If I were meant to have remembered, I would have.

So I have no shame.

I would prefer to have the money in my bank right now.

But clearly, I wasn't meant to. If I were meant to have the money, I would have it.

See where we're going here?

That $1062 credit will likely save me tens of thousands of dollars (not to mention unclaimed children) because of the memory hack I learned from my brother.

Which I wouldn't have learned if I'd been choosing to feel too embarrassed to tell him about it. Let's celebrate who we are —in all our glorious imperfections—just because it feels so much better.

And when we feel better, we really do do better.

Thank the person who wronged you this week

The magic of coaching is that I don't agree with your beliefs, or even our shared cultural norms. This enables me to help you find relief from the suffering that you are causing yourself. I do this by showing you that your perspectives (which most normal people will share) are optional, and aren't working for you if they make you feel tight and clenched.

Claire, a gifted healer, told me that a client cheated her. She wasn't paid for a phone session because the client cancelled her credit card, and wasn't responding to her emails. Claire was upset, and it wasn't because of the lost income. She was shocked and hurt because of what she decided the client's actions meant:

"She doesn't value my work.
I was taken advantage of.
She used me."

I'd also be upset if I thought someone had used me and taken advantage of me. But we really have no idea what this woman's intention was, and Claire's interpretation is only one of many possibilities.

Here's what I offered Claire:

Thank her.

Say, "Thank you, client, for teaching me that I should process payments before phone sessions."

"Thank you for all the money your teaching will save me over the life of my business."

Claire's voice softened immediately, although she took a while to open to the perspective I offered her. But when she did, our conversation turned to generating options for Claire to increase the efficiency of her growing business.

I taught her how to automate payments, contracts, and bookings. This freed her to see more clients and saved her thousands of dollars. More reasons to be grateful to her client—if not for her actions, Claire and I wouldn't have had this conversation because she hadn't seen her current policies as a problem!

It was a bit of a stretch for Claire to go to gratitude towards this woman. And I understand. Most normal people would agree with Claire that this a grave injustice and that she should find this woman and make her pay. Lucky for her that I'm not normal.

I'm not saying she shouldn't try to get paid if she can figure out how to do that, but I suggested that she constantly check in with herself to see how she's feeling while doing this. At the end of our call, Claire asked me—"So, should I send her another email" (to add to the emails she has so far not responded to)? I asked her how she felt when she thought about this. "Nah," she responded, "I would just be trying to make her feel guilty. Which feels tight and clenched to me."

I love this lesson:
"You can be happy or you can be right."

Claire could have hung onto her righteousness in this matter—no court would contest it. Or she could choose to find gratitude, compassion, and move on to giving herself her own happiness, which is worth much more than $150.

On being tested

I love love love how my life gives me moments where I get to consider and reaffirm everything that I hold to be important, and to gratefully celebrate that I am placing all my attention on exactly that.

The week we celebrated a coming of age ceremony for our youngest child was filled with wonderfulness for me.

We mark our children turning thirteen by celebrating the young people they are becoming. We wanted to make sure that we planned mindfully to make it a meaningful modeling for our children of what we consider to be important, which is family, values, and community. One of the ways we do this is to hold our celebrations in our home, which is quite unusual where we live.

Our home is on a quiet street, which makes it perfect for entertaining. Our back garden spills over into a glorious ravine, and we have a big deck overlooking the forest and a flower-filled front yard. We had planned to spread our guests around these three areas at tables covered with lavish silver tablecloths and delicious food. The caterers were going to place their food stations throughout the house and gardens, and we imagined a relaxed, informal event.

As you can imagine, hosting this event involved a lot of planning and running around, all of which we did, intentionally, with joy and lightness. Truly.

Many people expect us to be stressed and nervous before these events and we never are. We know that what's important is people, and as our celebrations always include people we love and who love us, we have never understood how they could ever be a source of stress.

This time we got tested. The week before the event, when I was driving around choosing balloons, decor, candy, desserts, centrepieces, outfits, shoes, etc., our van broke down. My husband waited over an hour in the hot sun for the tow truck to deliver the van to the service station, where we were told it would need almost $1000 of repairs. Then, three days before our event, the weather forecast, which was growing more and more ominous, switched from a likelihood of showers to a certainty thunderstorms...

We had no Plan B for the party, and 130 people in our house with caterers and food stations and bars would be unpleasantly crowded. We're not great believers in having Plan B's because we always believe that things will work out for us. And of course, they always do.

I chose to believe this:

"I am being tested and all I have to do to pass this test is to be pleasant to everyone and handle this all with grace."

And so, that's what I did.

My sister lent me her car.

We got the van fixed.

My sister came up with the brilliant idea of moving the party to the bright, airy school gym, where they provided us everything we needed for a stunning celebration, and family and friends stepped in to help us move everything. It remained a meaningful venue, as it's where my children have been nurtured and educated for the past 16 years and where we've met many of our closest friends.

Looking back, I honestly can't remember a moment of stress throughout all of this. My predominant thoughts were, "This is all working out exactly as it is meant to" and "The only thing that matters here are my people."

I was proud of my family. Not one of us made a fuss or even suggested that any of this was a problem. We all knew what was important, and none of that was affected by weather or unexpected expenses.

Who are you wasting your envy on?

DON'T WASTE YOUR ENVY

I arrived at my friend's house shortly after dinner one night. They were feeding their three young children and my six-year-old angel. Every plate on the table was empty.

I looked around enviously—the family ate the same meal at the same time? My friend laughed at me—that "same meal" was a conglomeration of 15 different customizations to please everyone's palate, and the 'wiped clean' plates were courtesy of their father, who efficiently consumed everyone's leftovers.

"A wasted envy," I said. She loved that concept.

Which got me thinking...How much energy do we expend on wasted envy?

Thin women?
I spent years envying them—one school mom in particular, who was the same age as me, had four kids like me, and also had a great body (unlike me). She recently, pulled me aside to ask about my weight loss coaching program.
Turns out her weekly beauty routine is: binge Friday to Sunday, starve Monday to Thursday, two-hour punishments at the gym Monday to Sunday. Intense fear every day.
How much energy did I use on that wasted envy?

Rich people?
My friend lives in an exclusive area of Toronto, filled with stately multimillion dollar homes. She thought she had been offended by a carpool mom, and decided to access her mortgage information out of spite. She discovered that this woman lives in a $3.48 million dollar home—which is mortgaged for $3 million.

How many people are wasting their envy on that family?

So tell me, who are you wasting your envy on? And how are you behaving when you're stuck in envy? For me, I would be likely to overeat in that moment to escape that poisonous envy.

Then I thought...what if everything I believed about these people was true?
Still a wasted envy.

What if she could eat whatever she wanted and maintain her gorgeous body?
Still a wasted envy.

What if they paid cash for their house and had tons more in the bank?
Still a wasted envy.

Any envy is wasted. It means I'm living in other people's business. Neglecting mine. Wasting my possibility for joy in that moment.

Good thing I know how to order up my feelings.

I know they're always caused by my thoughts, and I know how to direct my thinking to avoid wasting my precious life on envy.

And you can, too.

JEALOUSY

ENVY

Want to learn more about experiencing ease in your life?

Winters in Toronto are always cold. A few years ago we had unseasonably brutal weather, with icy winds, grey skies, and minus double-digit temperatures for weeks at a time. During those freezing weeks, I was grateful for my learned awareness that I have full power over my emotions.

Wherever I went, people blamed the weather for their misery. I heard them, but it was as if they were talking about an experience that I didn't share. Of course, we live in the same city, so I was experiencing the same temperatures. But not once did I feel tempted to believe that the wind chill could affect how I feel.

Only my thinking can affect my emotions. And I control what I focus on and think about. If I, like most people in Toronto, chose to think about the weather all the time, checked the weather every moment, and complained about it to everyone I saw, I would have been miserable for months.

Instead, I felt peaceful. For me, the weather is neutral. It's a number and it feels a certain way on my skin. That's it. All the rest is up to me.

While I may have felt physically cold this past winter, I took good care of myself because I know that how I feel is my responsibility.

A huge window.

I stayed home as much as possible, shopped where indoor parking was available, spent lots of time by my huge windows overlooking the ravine, and bundled up well when I went outside. And by not fighting with the weather I actually think I felt less cold.

Love always feels best

I was on the verge of tears when my husband left to take my daughter to school because we wouldn't be seeing each other for four nights. I counted.

It's ridiculous. He was here for weeks. Every night. And I barely paid any attention to him.

I had been indulging in resentment about the current effect of something he did years ago, and my way of 'punishing' him was to withdraw and withhold attention. I don't do it much anymore, but I guess it's a strong program in my brain, and I didn't even realize I was doing it until he left for a few days.

So here's the craziness: When he was here, I felt distant and uncaring. When he left, I felt tender love and appreciation.
This makes no sense, because he's the same guy. Always. One of my husband's qualities that makes him perfect for me is that his behaviour and moods are pretty constant, which is not something anyone would say about me.

This is what happens when we aren't paying attention to our minds and our hearts. We sink into old patterns, and they aren't always serving our highest purpose.

Choosing a regular practice of awareness is the antidote. When I take a few minutes every morning to decide who I want to be that day, I reset my program based on my highest desire, and it's always in the direction of love—in my heart and my actions. I forgot to do that regarding my husband for the past while.

The good news is that we are always offered reminders—we just need to be open to recognizing them. My sad heart that day was a reminder.

There's no purpose at all in regretting how I was the few weeks before he left because what we focus on is what we create more of. Instead, I focused on who I want to be towards him moving forward and then set a reminder in my heart to do more of that.

Because, honestly, love always feels the best.

About the author

Bev Aron

Bev Aron is a lifelong learner and a lover of "Big Talk" conversations (the opposite of small talk). She graduated with distinction from three universities, including a Masters from The London School of Economics and Political Science. However, her greatest and most rewarding challenge was completing her Master Coach Certification with The Life Coach School.

As The Deep Dive Coach, Bev coaches highly successful women who are involved in growth and healing work yet still struggle to find inner peace and achieve their wildest goals.

She also trains and mentors life coaches and master coaches at The Life Coach School.

Originally from Johannesburg, South Africa, Bev now lives in Toronto, Canada with her husband and four children.

Acknowledgements

A huge thank you to all the ones I love - my family, my business team, my book team, my coaches, clients, students, friends, teachers and mentors - you know who you are and I hope you know you have my enduring love and gratitude for making my world more than I could dream of every day.

References

Brown, B. (2015). Daring Greatly: How the Courage to Be Vulnerable Transforms the Way We Live, Love, Parent, and Lead. New York: Random House. (Referenced in this book on page 43 and page 62).

Castillo, B. (2009). Self-coaching 101: use your mind-- don't let it use you! United States: B. Castillo. (This book was my first encounter with Brooke Castillo, who became my coach, teacher, and mentor - I have since consumed everything she publishes, and my writing here is heavily influenced by her work. Referenced specifically on page 98 and 100)

Hendricks, G. (2010). The big leap: conquer your hidden fear and take life to the next level. New York: HarperCollins. (Referenced on page 86 in this book)

Hicks, E., & Hicks, J. (2007). The law of attraction. London: Hay House. (page 116 in this book)

Katie, S., & Mitchell, S. (2002). Loving what is: four questions that can change your life. New York: Harmony Books (I first encountered the idea that our minds are the obstacle in this book, which has influenced many of the thoughts I use to believe on purpose)

Rollo May, 1963, "Freedom and Responsibility Re-Examined" (Referenced on page 20 in this book)

Peale, N.V. (1905), "You Can If You Think You Can" New York: Touchstone (referenced on page 53 of this book)

Pressfield, S. (2003). The war of art. London: Orion. (Referenced on page 47 in this book)

Gallup & Rath, T. StrengthsFinder 2.0. Discover your Clifton Strengths.

Made in the USA
San Bernardino, CA
05 November 2019